T0276631

WOMEN
BEWARE
WOMEN

NEW MERMAIDS

General editor: Brian Gibbons
Professor of English Literature, University of Münster

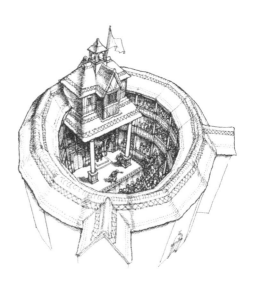

Reconstruction of an Elizabethan Theatre
by C. Walter Hodges

NEW MERMAIDS

NEW MERMAIDS

THOMAS MIDDLETON

WOMEN BEWARE WOMEN

edited by William C. Carroll
Boston University

BLOOMSBURY
LONDON • NEW DELHI • NEW YORK • SYDNEY

Bloomsbury Methuen Drama
An imprint of Bloomsbury Publishing Plc

50 Bedford Square	1385 Broadway
London	New York
WC1B 3DP	NY 10018
UK	USA

www.bloomsbury.com

Bloomsbury is a registered trade mark of Bloomsbury Publishing Plc

First New Mermaid edition 1968
© 1968 Ernest Benn Limited

Second edition 1994
Reprinted 1995, 1999
Reprinted with new cover 2002

© 1968 A & C Black Publishers Limited

All rights reserved. No part of this publication may be reproduced or transmitted
in any form or by any means, electronic or mechanical, including photocopying,
recording, or any information storage or retrieval system, without prior
permission in writing from the publishers.

No responsibility for loss caused to any individual or organization acting on or
refraining from action as a result of the material in this publication
can be accepted by Bloomsbury or the author.

All rights whatsoever in this play are strictly reserved and application for performance
etc. should be made before rehearsals by professionals and by amateurs to the
publisher. Mail to: Performance.permissions@bloomsbury.com. No performance
may be given unless a licence has been obtained.

No rights in incidental music or songs contained in the work are hereby granted
and performance rights for any performance/presentation whatsoever
must be obtained from the respective copyright owners.

Visit www.bloomsbury.com to find out more about our authors and their books
You will find extracts, author interviews, author events and you can sign up for
newsletters to be the first to hear about our latest releases and special offers.

British Library Cataloguing-in-Publication Data
A catalogue record for this book is available from the British Library.

ISBN: PB:	978-0-7136-6663-2
EPDF:	978-1-4081-4459-6
EPUB:	978-1-4081-4460-2

Library of Congress Cataloging-in-Publication Data
A catalog record for this book is available from the Library of Congress.

CONTENTS

ACKNOWLEDGEMENTS

I have drawn gratefully on the work of previous editors of this play, especially the earlier New Mermaid edition by Roma Gill, as well as the Revels edition by J. R. Mulryne, the Cambridge edition by David L. Frost, and the Penguin edition by Bryan Loughrey and Neil Taylor.

I am especially indebted to four generous colleagues – Keir Elam, Scott Cutler Shershow, James R. Siemon and David P. Young – for their assistance at various stages of this project; their wisdom and advice have been as valuable as their friendship, which is saying a great deal.

ABBREVIATIONS

I have followed the standard practice of referring to the first edition of *Women Beware Women* – the 1657 octavo – as O. Modern editions are referred to as follows:

Dyce	*The Works of Thomas Middleton*, edited by Alexander Dyce (1840)
Bullen	*The Works of Thomas Middleton*, edited by A. H. Bullen (1885–6)
Gill	*Women Beware Women*, edited by Roma Gill (New Mermaid, London, 1968)
Barber	*Women Beware Women*, edited by Charles Barber (Fountainwell Drama Texts, Berkeley, 1969)
Mulryne	*Women Beware Women*, edited by J. R. Mulryne (Revels, Manchester, 1975)
Frost	*The Selected Plays of Thomas Middleton*, edited by David L. Frost (Cambridge, 1978)
Loughrey and Taylor	*Thomas Middleton: Five Plays*, edited by Bryan Loughrey and Neil Taylor (London, 1988)

Other works frequently referred to are abbreviated as:

Holdsworth	R. V. Holdsworth, 'Thomas Middleton: *Women Beware Women*', *RES*, n.s. 29 (1978), 88–93
Jonson	*Ben Jonson*, edited by C. H. Herford and Percy and Evelyn Simpson (Oxford, 1925–52)
Tilley	M. P. Tilley, *A Dictionary of the Proverbs in England* (Ann Arbor, 1950)

Names of periodicals are abbreviated as:

CE	*Cahiers Elisabéthains*
ELR	*English Literary Renaissance*
JEGP	*Journal of English and Germanic Philology*
Lib	*The Library*
MLN	*Modern Language Notes*
MLR	*Modern Language Review*
MP	*Modern Philology*
PLL	*Papers on Language and Literature*
PQ	*Philological Quarterly*

RES	*Review of English Studies*
RMS	*Renaissance and Modern Studies* (University of Nottingham)
RORD	*Research Opportunities in Renaissance Drama*
SEL	*Studies in English Literature*
SIcon	*Studies in Iconography*
SP	*Studies in Philology*
TSE	*Tulane Studies in English*
YES	*Yearbook of English Studies*

Quotations from Shakespeare are from *The Complete Works of Shakespeare* (Fourth Edition), edited by David Bevington (New York, 1992). Quotations from other plays (except those of Jonson) are from the New Mermaid editions.

INTRODUCTION

THE AUTHOR

THOMAS MIDDLETON lived and worked in London nearly all his life.[1] Born in 1580, he was christened at St Lawrence Jewry on 18 April, and was buried on 4 July 1627 at his parish church in Newington Butts, where he had lived from at least 1609. His father, William, was a bricklayer and gentleman with his own coat of arms; he died in January 1585/86, and in November 1586 his widow, Anne, married Thomas Harvey, who had just returned, impoverished, from a voyage to Virginia. Within weeks of the marriage, Harvey was revealed to be an unscrupulous adventurer, almost solely interested in gaining control of his wife's estate. A protracted, confusing and ugly series of lawsuits engulfed the family over the next two decades, all beginning with Harvey's attempt to take over the property which Anne had put in trust for her children before she met him. Allen Waterer, who married Middleton's sister, Avis, in 1596, immediately became a party to the lawsuits as well. By 1603, when both Anne Harvey and Allen Waterer died, Middleton had spent a good part of his time assisting his mother in the various legal battles. Even after Waterer's death, Avis and her second husband, John Empson, continued legal action over the family property.

Middleton's life was early and frequently connected to the professional theatre. A large part of the family property at question in the various lawsuits was 'the grounde called the Curteyn where now comenlye the Playes be playde' – that is, the Curtain Theatre (built in 1577). After matriculating at Queen's College, Oxford (the most popular college of the time) in April 1598, moreover, Middleton was forced in June 1600 to convey his half-share of the Curtain property to his brother-in-law Waterer for money 'paid and disbursed for my advauncement & preferment in the university of Oxford where I am nowe a student'. Some time during the next eight months, however, he had to return to London to deal with the continuing series of lawsuits, and it was reported, as of 8 February 1600/1, that Middleton 'remaynethe heare in London daylie accompaninge the players'. In a final

[1] The chief facts of Middleton's life have been set forth in two articles by Mark Eccles: 'Middleton's Birth and Education', *RES* 7 (1931), 431–41, and ' "Thomas Middleton A Poett" ', *SP* 54 (1957), 516–36. Virtually all the facts in this commentary derive from Eccles. I have also found useful R. C. Bald, 'Middleton's Civic Employments', *MP* 31 (1933), 65–78; Mildred G. Christian, 'A Sidelight on the Family History of Thomas Middleton', *SP* 44 (1947), 490–6; and P. G. Phialas, 'Middleton's Early Contact with the Law', *SP* 52 (1955), 186–94.

twist, Middleton's brother-in-law, Thomas Marbeck, was an actor for the Admiral's Men; Middleton thus may have met his wife through this association. Middleton in any event never graduated from Oxford, and was already a professional playwright at the time he would have been receiving his diploma.

Since his son Edward was aged nineteen in 1623, we assume Middleton was married about 1602. His wife, Magdalen (she is 'Maria' or Mary in one document), was the granddaughter of the famous composer and organist John Marbeck; Eccles believes she was probably the Maulyn Marbeck christened on 9 July 1575 at St Dunstan's in the West. Middleton's widow petitioned in February 1627/28 for a gift of money from the city of London, which suggests that his estate had been small. She died five months later, in July 1628, and was also buried at Newington.

Middleton published one book of verse, *The Wisdom of Solomon Paraphrased* (1597), before he entered Oxford, and two more, *Micro-Cynicon* (1599) and the *Ghost of Lucrece* (1600), while presumably still a student. In 1602 Henslowe recorded that he was working on three plays: a collaboration with Dekker, Munday, Drayton and Webster on *Caesar's Fall* (now lost); *Randal, Earl of Chester* (also lost); and an unnamed play. Two years later, in 1604, he published two satiric prose pieces, *The Black Book* and *The Ant and the Nightingale*. His earliest surviving play, *The Family of Love* (c. 1602–3), also dates from this period. If the quality of these early works is debatable, it is clear that, after he left Oxford, Middleton was both an active and a highly productive writer. Beginning in 1613 and continuing until his death, he also wrote a number of civic pageants and entertainments; as early as 1604, he had written a speech given as part of Dekker's *The Magnificent Entertainment* for King James's official entry into London. Middleton was appointed City Chronologer in 1620, to record the memorable acts and occurrences of the city; he was succeeded in this position by Ben Jonson.

Middleton wrote in a variety of genres, but his greatest achievements came in two distinct dramatic forms: (1) city comedies, including *Michaelmas Term* (c. 1605), *A Mad World, My Masters* (c. 1605), *A Trick to Catch the Old One* (c. 1606) and *A Chaste Maid in Cheapside* (c. 1611–13); and (2) tragedies, including *The Revenger's Tragedy* (c. 1606–7), *Women Beware Women* (c. 1621) and *The Changeling*, with William Rowley (1622). Middleton's accomplishments in tragicomedy – *The Witch* (c. 1615), *A Fair Quarrel* (c. 1615–17) and *The Old Law* (1618), among others – were also substantial. In 1624 he wrote the political satire *A Game at Chess*, which had the longest consecutive run of any play in the Jacobean period (indeed, the first long run in English

theatrical history), nine days at the Globe, and caused a sensation
in London; the play was finally suppressed by the government,
though it had been properly licensed. Middleton and the players
were summoned before the Privy Council (his son Edward
answered for him, as Middleton seems to have been lying low),
but no action was taken.

Middleton wrote for the children's companies of Paul's and
Blackfriars, and after they disbanded, for Prince Henry's
(formerly the Admiral's) Men, the Lady Elizabeth's company,
and for Shakespeare's company, the King's Men. He collaborated
on plays with many other dramatists of the period, possibly with
Shakespeare himself on *Timon of Athens*, and seems to have
revised Shakespeare's *Macbeth* some years after its first performance.[2] From his inheritance in The Curtain to his pageants
for the city, Middleton's whole life traces the arc of the recently
invented career of the professional playwright.

DATE AND SOURCES

There is no record of *Women Beware Women* until long after
Middleton's death: it was entered in the Stationers' Register in
1653, and published in 1657. In his commendatory poem
(usually dated *c.* 1640) to the 1657 edition, Nathaniel Richards
mentions seeing it performed, but does not say when; no other
contemporary reference to the play exists. Dating the play must
therefore be done by internal evidence and by a sense of Middleton's canon and development. Scholarly opinion has focussed
on two possibilities: a relatively early date (1613–14), though
one after Middleton had already written several extraordinary
plays; and a late date (*c.* 1621), placing the play just before *The
Changeling*.

The argument for the earlier date, advanced most recently by
J. I. Cope[3], is based on a few similarities between *Women* and the
masque *The Triumphs of Truth* (1613); earlier arguments by Fleay
and Schelling for this date were based on an alleged allusion to
a Dekker masque of 1612.[4] None of these parallels is particularly
convincing, and few scholars now agree with either theory.

The argument for the later date is based on not much greater
evidence. *Women* alludes to the Virginia Company, which was

---

[2] The Oxford Shakespeare editors, Stanley Wells and Gary Taylor, have most recently
advanced these arguments.
[3] J. I. Cope, 'The Date of Middleton's *Women Beware Women*', *MLN* 76 (1961), 295–
300
[4] Mulryne, p. xxxiii

highly topical in 1621, but so too does *The Roaring Girl*, published in 1611. The Duke's age – 'about some fifty-five' (I.iii.92) – would have coincided with James I's age in 1621; but Holdsworth points out Middleton's 'odd fancy for the number fifty-five', noting its use in five other works, dating from 1604.[5] Another argument once advanced was that Sir Henry Herbert, who became Master of the Revels in 1622, kept note of the plays he licensed for performance, and *Women Beware Women* is not listed – suggesting that it was performed prior to 1622; but only a selection of Herbert's office-book was ever printed.[6] Middleton's apparent use of Fynes Morison's *Itinerary* (*c.* 1619–20) as a source also points to the later date. Finally, Middleton may be alluding to a line from *Swetnam the Woman-hater* in his title (see the discussion below); that play was performed *c.* 1618, and published in 1620. The evidence is admittedly slight, but what there is points to a date *c.* 1621, and most modern editors agree. The preference for the later date is usually also based on a sense that the play reflects a style and sophistication similar to that of *The Changeling*.

Middleton's main source for the story of Bianca and the Duke was *novelle* 84 and 85 of Celio Malespini's *Ducento Novelle* (Venice, 1609). The main outlines of the story adopted as the plot of *Women Beware Women* are clear enough: Bianca Capello, a Venetian heiress, falls in love with Pietro, a bank clerk, and elopes with him to Florence. There she is seen by the Grand Duke Francesco, who falls in love with her, and – with the aid of his friend Mondragone's wife – surprises Bianca in Mondragone's house and offers her his protection and comfort. In Malespini's account, no rape or force is involved: after many conversations, he says, 'Bianca at length consented to bestow her love on the enamoured Grand Duke. Her indulgence of this passion, and her most happy familiarity [with the Duke], she increased from day to day. Mutual love grew between them'.[7] Bianca's husband, Pietro, accepts his cuckoldry, but eventually boasts that he is the lover of Cassandra, a wealthy widow; her outraged family complains to the Duke, who arranges Pietro's murder. Bianca's grief over his death is consoled by the Duke.

The story of Bianca and the Duke was also briefly told by Fynes Moryson, in his *Itinerary* (completed *c.* 1619–20, though not published until 1903); Middleton's use of Moryson is highly probable. Moryson continues the story beyond Malespini's

---

[5] R. V. Holdsworth, '*Women Beware Women* and *The Changeling* on the Stage', in *Three Jacobean Revenge Tragedies: A Casebook*, ed. R. V. Holdsworth (London, 1990), p. 248

[6] G. E. Bentley, *The Jacobean and Caroline Stage* (Oxford, 1956), IV.906

[7] Quoted from Mulryne's translation, p. 173

account with the entrance of the Duke's brother, the Cardinal: Bianca sends him poisoned marzipan, but when he sends it back untouched, the Duke meets the messenger and eats a piece of it. Hearing that the Duke has eaten of it, Bianca 'with an unchanged Countenance tooke another peece, and having eaten it, locked herself in a clossett, and hereupon the Duke and shee dyed in one hower'.[8]

Still a third source for the play is a short novel, published in 1628, entitled *The True History of the Tragicke Loves of Hipolito and Isabella Neapolitans*, which tells the basic story of the Hippolito-Isabella sub-plot, with Hippolito's sister a nun. Middleton could have read the novel in manuscript, or he could have read the original version (published in 1597) in French. The correspondences are so extensive, at any rate, that there is no doubt that Middleton used the *True History* in one version or another.

Middleton thus took a good deal of his plot from these sources, but the most distinctive scenes in the play – the chess scene, the Ward's inspection of Isabella, the masque scene – are Middleton's own invention. Similarly, perhaps his most memorable character, Livia, a composite of different figures in the sources, is also his own creation. Finally, it is worth noting that Middleton makes the Duke's encounter with Bianca in the chess scene far more threatening and sinister than it is in his sources.

THE PLAY

Women Beware Women has increasingly been recognized as a major achievement of tragic drama. While Middleton was 'clearly not ranked with Jonson or Shakespeare' in his lifetime[9] (Ben Jonson called him a 'base fellow'),[10] and his work fell into relative neglect until the later nineteenth century, his reputation in general, and for *Women Beware Women* in particular, has risen substantially since – and to some extent, in spite of – T. S. Eliot's essay in 1927.[11] Scholarly consensus now ranks Middleton and

---

[8] Quoted from Gill, p. xv

[9] Sara Jayne Steen, 'The Response to Middleton: His Own Time to Eliot', *RORD* 28 (1985), p. 65. See also the useful companion piece in the same volume by Geraldo U. de Sousa, 'Thomas Middleton: Criticism since T. S. Eliot'.

[10] Jonson, I.137

[11] Eliot remarked that: 'Of all the Elizabethan dramatists Middleton seems the most impersonal, the most indifferent to personal fame or perpetuity, the readiest, except Rowley, to accept collaboration... He remains merely a name, a voice, the author of certain plays, which are all of them great plays. He has no point of view, is neither sentimental nor cynical; he is neither resigned, nor disillusioned, nor romantic, he has no message. He is merely the name which associates six or seven great plays' (*Selected Essays of T. S. Eliot* (New York, 1960), pp. 140–1).

Ben Jonson as the major playwrights, after Shakespeare, of the
English Renaissance. The chief authorizing document hitherto
lacking in Middleton's case – a modern, scholarly edition of all
his works – will be provided by the imminent publication of a
collected works. Since the joint or sole authorship of several texts
remains in dispute,[12] there will be further debate about the extent
and identity of Middleton's canon, but there can no longer
be serious doubt about Middleton's range, productivity and
achievement. It is already clear that Middleton's three great
tragedies – *The Revenger's Tragedy* (1607), *Women Beware Women*
(1621) and *The Changeling* (1622) – rank him with Marlowe,
Shakespeare and Webster as pre-eminent in his time for tragedy.

Nathaniel Richards provides the only seventeenth-century evidence that *Women Beware Women* was actually staged, and was a
success: 'I that have seen't can say, having just cause, / Never
came tragedy off with more applause'. Yet while he refers to the
play simply as a 'tragedy', recent criticism, though agreeing in
its general estimation, shows little agreement about just what
kind of tragedy it is. Schoenbaum credits the play with verging
on the creation of 'a novel kind of drama – a drama that occupies
a middle ground between comedy and tragedy'.[13] And in this
vein, the play has recently been classified as a 'realistic bourgeois
tragedy', a 'city tragedy', a 'tragedy of judgment', 'an *anticourt*
tragedy written from a citizen's perspective' and a 'domestic
tragedy'.[14] It is said both to have 'many affinities with satiric
comedy', and to begin 'where a romantic comedy might have
ended'.[15] Nicholas Brooke concludes, more radically, that in
Women Beware Women Middleton 'demonstrates the absurdity of
worshipping tragedy as a moral force'.[16] Even the play's title –
taken straightforwardly by earlier generations of scholars – now

---

[12] On the composition of Middleton's literary canon, see David J. Lake, *The Canon of
Thomas Middleton's Plays* (Cambridge, 1975) and M. P. Jackson, *Studies in Attribution:
Middleton and Shakespeare* (Salzburg, 1979). The overwhelming scholarly consensus
now is that *The Revenger's Tragedy*, once attributed to Tourneur, is by Middleton.

[13] Samuel Schoenbaum, *Middleton's Tragedies* (New York, 1955), p. 130

[14] These assessments are by, respectively, Robert Ornstein, *The Moral Vision of Jaco-
bean Tragedy* (Madison, WI, 1960), p. 192; Margot Heinemann, *Puritanism and
Theatre: Thomas Middleton and Opposition Drama under the Early Stuarts* (Cambridge,
1980), p. 172; Albert H. Tricomi, *Anticourt Drama in England 1603–1642*
(Charlottesville, VA, 1989), p. 128; Tricomi, p. 121; and Robert N. Watson, in *The
Cambridge Companion to English Renaissance Drama*, ed. A. R. Braunmuller and
Michael Hattaway (Cambridge, 1990), p. 313.

[15] Alexander Leggatt, *English Drama: Shakespeare to the Restoration, 1590–1660*
(London, 1988), p. 147; Inga-Stina Ewbank, 'The Middle of Middleton', in *The
Arts of Performance in Elizabethan and Early Stuart Drama*, ed. Murray Biggs et al.
(Edinburgh, 1991), p. 169

[16] Nicholas Brooke, *Horrid Laughter in Jacobean Tragedy* (London, 1979), p. 110

seems generically problematic: the title is said to be, variously, 'misleading', possibly 'conceived in a spirit of parody', perhaps 'a comedy title' or 'shar[ing] the ambivalence' of the rest of the play.[17] The modern critical history of *Women Beware Women* may suggest a generic incoherence or instability, perhaps resulting from the dramatist's own 'ambivalence' of values. It may also be argued, however, that it is not that the dramatist's values are ambivalent, but that the values traditionally inherent in the genre of tragedy no longer seemed plausible or sustainable in the London of the 1620s.

The title's irony (or lack of it) may be clarified if one accepts the likelihood that it echoes a speech by Misogynos in the anonymous play *Swetnam the Woman-hater* (c. 1618; published 1620):[18]

> And Fortune, if thou be'st a deitie,
> Give me but opportunitie, that I
> May all the follies of your Sex declare,
> That henceforth Men of Women may beware.   (III.ii.90–3)

A vigorous dialogue – or rather, shouting match – between misogynist literature and defences of women may be traced back to the Middle Ages; but it had been re-energized in the early Renaissance, when new theories concerning the education of women were debated in Humanist writings.[19] The social and political events of the previous decade, then, particularly the revival of the women's controversy, could have had as much to do with an evolving conception of the dramatic subject as any

---

[17] These assessments are by, respectively, Ornstein, p. 191; J. B. Batchelor, 'The Pattern of *Women Beware Women*', *YES* 2 (1972), p. 81; Leggatt, *English Drama*, p. 147; and Anthony B. Dawson, '*Women Beware Women* and the Economy of Rape', *SEL* 27 (1987), 311.

[18] Mulryne, p. xxxvi, makes this suggestion. The quotation is from Coryl Crandall, *Swetnam the Woman-hater: The Controversy and the Play, A Critical Edition with Introduction and Notes* (Purdue, 1969).

[19] The best single study of the debate in the Renaissance is by Linda Woodbridge, *Women and the English Renaissance: Literature and the Nature of Womankind, 1540–1620* (Urbana, Ill., 1984). The first work to offer an extended argument for seeing the play in this context was Caroline Lockett Cherry, *The Most Unvaluedst Purchase: Women in The Plays of Thomas Middleton* (Salzburg, 1973); virtually no one, however, has followed up on her argument. Ingrid Hotz-Davies, in '*A Chaste Maid in Cheapside* and *Women Beware Women*: Feminism, Anti-feminism, and the Limitations of Satire', *CE* 39 (1991), 29–39, briefly rejects some of Cherry's conclusions about Middleton's own ideological position, arguing that he undermines all the 'feminist' commentary in the play.

conjectural psychological ambivalence in Middleton himself.[20]

The controversy in England over a woman's place became sharply focussed during the Reformation, as largely Protestant ideas – of a woman's right to choose her own husband, of a woman's relative equality within marriage, of the possibility of divorce – came into widespread conflict with the medieval tradition. Queen Elizabeth's ascent to the throne (1558) and eventual political dominance added contradictory ingredients to the debate: Elizabeth was, on the one hand, the Virgin Queen, the quintessence of the feminine; yet she also claimed to have the soul of a man, and preserved her virginity partly because she would not surrender her political power as the head of one hierarchical system for the domestic subjection of another. During the reign of James I the voices of controversy were even more frequent and strident. In *The Roaring Girl* (*c.* 1608–11), Middleton (with Dekker) reflects an awareness of these contemporary debates, particularly the king's own condemnations of women dressed as men. In the years immediately preceding the writing of *Women Beware Women*, however, the controversy became extremely pointed and topical. In 1615 Joseph Swetnam's *The Arraignment of Lewd, Idle, Froward, and Unconstant Women*, a bilious misogynist attack, launched a pamphlet war. Swetnam's attack was highly popular (ten editions had been published by 1637), and was quickly followed by defences of women by Daniel Tuvil in *Asylum Veneris* (1616), Rachel Speght in *A Muzzle for Melastomus* (1617), Esther Sowernam in *Esther Hath Hanged Haman* (1617) and Constantia Munda in *The Worming of a Mad Dog* (1617). All but Tuvil directly refer to Swetnam. Finally, the anonymous play *Swetnam the Woman-hater* was written around 1618. As James himself attacked women's style of dress, two further pamphlets appeared in 1620: *Hic Mulier; or, the Man-Woman* and *Haec Vir; or, the Womanish Man*. In that same year, John Chamberlain commented to Sir Dudley Carleton on the extent and virulence of the controversy: 'Our pulpits ring continually of the insolence and impudence of women: and to help the matter forward, the players have likewise taken them to task, and so too the ballads and ballad-singers, so that they can come nowhere but their ears tingle. And, if all this will not serve, the King threatens to fall upon their husbands, parents, or friends, that have, or should have power over them,

[20] The important books by Heinemann and Tricomi have gone far to establish other social and political contexts of Middleton's work. Heinemann demonstrates the often surprising Puritan context – Middleton was said to be the Puritans' favourite dramatist – and Tricomi describes how *Women Beware Women* participates in a more general 'anticourt' discourse.

and make them pay for it'.[21] It was in this context, then, that
Middleton wrote *Women Beware Women*.

The play takes up several issues central to the contemporary
women's controversy, especially the arranged or enforced marriage and the right of women to choose their husband.[22] When
Fabritio insists Isabella must marry the Ward, Livia corrects him:

> Oh soft there, brother! Though you be a Justice,
> Your warrant cannot be served out of your liberty.
> You may compel, out of the power of father,
> Things merely harsh to a maid's flesh and blood,
> But when you come to love, there the soil alters;
> Y'are in another country.   (I.ii.131–6)

Isabella's plight was a familiar one in Jacobean drama, which
frequently depicted the evils of enforced marriage:

>   Oh the heart-breakings
> Of miserable maids, where love's enforced!
> The best condition is but bad enough:
> When women have their choices, commonly
> They do but buy their thraldoms, and bring great portions
> To men to keep 'em in subjection –
>   . . .
>   By'r Lady, no misery surmounts a woman's!
> Men buy their slaves, but women buy their masters.
>   (I.ii.166–71, 175–6)

As Bianca remarks to Mother,

> Wives do not give away themselves to husbands,
> To the end to be quite cast away; they look
> To be the better used, and tendered rather,
> Highlier respected, and maintained the richer;
> They're well rewarded else for the free gift
> Of their whole life to a husband,   (III.i.47–52)

so (in a passage quoted below) she also rejects the close, pos-
sessive confinement of young girls as counterproductive, and in
any case futile. Livia – her very character being perhaps the
greatest testament to Middleton's interest in the condition of
women – articulates the classic double standard of a patriarchal
society:

> FABRITIO   Why, is not man
>   Tied to the same observance, lady sister,
>   And in one woman?
> LIVIA   'Tis enough for him;

[21] *The Letters of John Chamberlain*, ed. N. E. McClure (Philadelphia, 1939), II.289
[22] For other dramatic examples, see Glenn H. Blayney, 'Enforcement of Marriage in
English Drama (1600–1650)', *PQ* 38 (1959), 459–72.

> Besides, he tastes of many sundry dishes
> That we poor wretches never lay our lips to –
> As obedience, forsooth, subjection, duty, and such kickshaws,
> All of our making, but served in to them.   (I.ii.37–43)

Such complaints and pleas for women's freedom in *Women
Beware Women* are intense, but they are also all compromised
and subverted even as they are expressed. Isabella's rejection of
enforced marriage may be compelling, especially given the
Ward's brutal idiocy, but it also serves as a rationalization for an
adulterous liaison with Hippolito. Livia's often witty defiance of
the constrictions of female convention may make her an attractive
figure, almost another Beatrice, yet she uses her freedom to play
the bawd for the Duke and Bianca, and does even worse to
Isabella with her false story.[23] Bianca herself, once she is raped,
turns willing adulteress and murderess. Middleton's sympathy
for these women seems genuine, and he reveals how they often
act on unconscious motivations they cannot recognize or control,
but the play also understands how subjection and weakness can
turn to special pleading, sexual licence and violence. Livia wants
equality for women, but in all the wrong things: a man may taste
of 'many sundry dishes', she argues,

> And if we lick a finger then sometimes
> We are not to blame: your best cooks use it.   (I.ii.44–5)

Those who are subjected and victimized, it appears, simply want
a chance at running the same hypocritical game.

Middleton's title therefore suggests that the play represents a
deliberate intervention in a contentious contemporary discourse,
one that had a direct connection to the 'subject' of tragedy – that
genre in which the organs of increase always dry up. If there is
one thing predictable about the tragic drama of the English
Renaissance, it is that the women will all be dead at the end. In
Middleton's play, women must beware of men as much as of
women; Livia is horribly destructive, but no less so than the
patriarchal structure of society as a whole. The warning to beware
of women, after all, derives from Misogynos himself. Perhaps we
should also hear in the title a less directed warning: Women,
beware! Women!

Middleton has, from the beginning, always been praised for
his creation of memorable, psychologically complex female
characters. Nathaniel Richards's commendatory verse singles
out this quality: 'He knew the rage, / Madness of women crossed;

---

[23] For a useful study of Livia, see Kenneth Muir, 'The Role of Livia in "Women
Beware Women" ', in *Poetry and Drama 1570–1700*, ed. Antony Coleman and Antony
Hammond (London, 1981).

and for the stage / Fitted their humours, hell-bred malice, strife / Acted in state, presented to the life'. Rather like Misogynos, Richards singles out the destructive energies of Middleton's women, also remarking on the 'plots, poisons, mischiefs that seldom miss / To murder virtue with a venom kiss', but he also, however tentatively, registers some of the causes for their violence and fury: the murderous 'drabs of state' are 'vexed', the mad women 'crossed'. In this same tradition, Una Ellis-Fermor's comment of 1935 became the authorized version of praise: 'Middleton's capacity for tragedy is inseparable from his other supreme gift, his discernment of the minds of women; in this no dramatist of the period except Shakespeare is his equal'.[24]

Such panegyric has frequently accompanied discussions of Middleton as a realist, or 'merely a great recorder' of life, in Eliot's phrase, a kind of 'seventeenth century Ibsen'.[25] Middleton's representation of female psychology, however, no longer appears as such an isolated phenomenon; it can now be seen, rather, to be inextricably linked to a recognition of women's social and economic positions in a patriarchal society. *Women Beware Women* exposes the destructive effects of the commodification of women as powerfully as anything in Jacobean literature. His female characters openly reflect on their exploitation and appropriation by men and the culture men have created – and some of them turn their subjection into a weapon of malice. 'They are the creatures of their environment', Margot Heinemann has noted, 'as well as of original sin'.[26] Thus, the nature of Middleton's 'realism' has been readjusted in recent criticism, from that of the precursor to Ibsen who brought us memorable women and realistic social detail, to that of the sympathetic dramatist who also understood that 'the best condition', for most women, 'is but bad enough'.

Nicholas Brooke has claimed that Middleton was 'the most controlled artist' of the Jacobean dramatists, and the carefully articulated structure of *Women Beware Women* reflects his claim.[27] The play enacts an ascent of class, social custom, and hierarchy which is simultaneous with, and indistinguishable from, a debilitating moral decline.[28] It is impossible to say which is cause and

---

[24] Una Ellis-Fermor, *The Jacobean Drama* (New York, 1964), p. 149

[25] Eliot, *Selected Essays*, p. 148; G. R. Hibbard, 'The Tragedies of Thomas Middleton and the Decadence of the Drama', *RMS* 1 (1957), p. 54

[26] *Puritanism and Theatre*, p. 191   [27] Brooke, *Horrid Laughter*, p. 110

[28] Batchelor ('Pattern', p. 84) first briefly observed this progression, but Brooke offers a fuller and richer description. See also John Potter, ' "In Time of Sports": Masques and Masking in Middleton's *Women Beware Women*', *PLL* 18 (1982), for an interesting argument that 'public festivals' are the 'essential organizing principle of the play' (p. 368).

which effect. The play opens in Leantio's house; he is a 'factor', a low-level commercial agent, and the values associated with him and his house in the first scene are commercial and bourgeois. The site of the second scene, Fabritio's house, technically constitutes a rise on the social scale, but in reality there is little to differentiate it from Leantio's house. Act I, scene iii moves outside Leantio's house for the first time, with catastrophic results, when the progress of the Duke and the nobility of Florence passes in the street. The second and third acts of the play move entirely to Livia's house (except for the final return in III.i to Leantio's house). Livia's house is clearly yet another notch higher on the social scale. Here the Mother may visit but she feels out of place; here the Duke can be entertained, and aristocratic games of chess and seduction can be discreetly played out. When Bianca returns for the play's final visit to Leantio's house in III.i, it has become 'the strangest house' (l. 16), no longer in her view a place of middle-class comfort but one of *déclassé* confinement; Leantio's first thought, on hearing that the Duke has seen Bianca at the window, is to ask 'Is the door fast?' and to propose the 'conveyance' 'at the end of the dark parlour' where he would, too late, 'lock my life's best treasure up' (ll. 240–6). In the return to Livia's house in III.ii, Bianca arrives not with Leantio but with the Duke, and is now openly his mistress. Acts IV and V complete the play's social ascent by first placing Bianca in the Duke's palace, with the regal marriage procession in IV.iii confirming her new status, and then installing her 'above' with the Duke and the rest of the nobility. This social trajectory is marked by acute observation on Middleton's part: clothing, possessions, imagery and rhetoric are all carefully calibrated to register social difference. Even the loutish Ward, as Brooke has noted, 'is usefully as well as symbolically placed below stairs' in the final scene.[29]

Middleton's precise manipulation of the play's social setting corresponds of course with Bianca's social rise to marriage with the Duke, but it also corresponds with an equally precise employment of the upper stage, as Marjorie S. Lancaster has demonstrated. Arguing that Middleton's use of the upper stage reflects 'his characters' inverted morality', Lancaster demonstrates the recurrent irony in the play's 'placement of the two lovers, one positioned on the upper stage and the other below' in three crucial scenes.[30] Thus, Bianca is 'above' with the Mother and the Duke is below in I.iii, when he first sees her. In the

[29] Brooke, *Horrid Laughter*, p. 97
[30] 'Middleton's Use of the Upper Stage in *Women Beware Women*', *TSE* 22 (1977), pp. 70, 73

famous chess scene of II.ii, Bianca enters below but is led above, where she is surprised by the Duke. Finally, Bianca enters 'above' with the Duke and the entire court in the final scene; they view the court masque, staged below, while seated above. Bianca and the Duke thus act out a demonic parody of the lovers' elevation in *Romeo and Juliet*. (Whether they die on the upper stage or descend to the main stage is unclear.)[31]

The play's social and physical progressions develop simultaneously with morally debilitating regressions. Bianca, again, is at the centre of them. The very young girl ('about sixteen', III.i.180) of the first act, who ran away and married for love, is 'strangely altered' (III.i.7) by the third act, and in the fourth act is a 'glist'ring whore' (IV.ii.20), in Leantio's words, fully capable of turning the language of Christian charity back against the Cardinal while secretly plotting his murder by poison in the final scene. To say that Bianca's morality 'descends' while her social position 'ascends' in the play is a useful enough formulation of the play's strategy, but such a formulation does not adequately represent the deep identity of these processes. The play is not simply a study of moral loss, as earlier commentators tended to argue, but also a study of the social conditions which permit, perhaps even generate, the moral chaos of the play.

There is one final simultaneous 'descent', which other commentators have not, to my knowledge, previously mentioned: the play articulates an ugly escalation in sexual violence against women. Marriage to Bianca is exhilarating for Leantio, but it is also a 'sin . . . the best piece of theft / That ever was committed', yet pardoned, he believes, through marriage (I.i.35, 43–4). A figurative rape, in short, in the same sense that Saturninus terms Bassianus's seizure of Lavinia in *Titus Andronicus* a 'rape', to which Bassianus replies, ' "Rape" call you it, my lord, to seize my own, / My true-betrothed love and now my wife? / But let the laws of Rome determine all; / Meanwhile am I possessed of that is mine' (*Titus Andronicus* I.i.405–9). Like Shakespeare, Middleton reveals the male 'possession' of the female body in marriage to be a form of rape. The commodification of the female body – Leantio calls Bianca a 'purchase' (12), a 'treasure' (14) a 'masterpiece' (41) and a 'jewel' (162) in the first scene alone – makes it a potential site of violence; objectified thus, it may be seized, locked up, put on display, fingered and inspected, penetrated.

[31] Leslie Thomson, in ' "*Enter Above*": The Staging of *Women Beware Women*', *SEL* 26 (1986), has argued that the court party must come down to the lower stage in the final part of the scene, for both symbolic and practical reasons; she also argues that the Cardinal must descend as well, a more debatable proposition.

Middleton's play also follows *Titus* (I am not suggesting any direct influence) in matching this opening marriage/rape with an actual rape just before the middle of the play. In an important article, Anthony Dawson has thoroughly examined what he terms 'the economy of rape' in *Women Beware Women*, seeing rape as 'an emblem of hierarchy', and he exhorts that we 'first rid ourselves of the idea that the Duke's action constitutes a seduction (which is what virtually every critic calls it) rather than a rape'. Middleton, he argues, 'locates the issue where it belongs – in the area of power relations', and leaves the question of consent ambiguous.[32]

The site of the Duke's assault on Bianca is the famous chess scene (II.ii), its lower-stage chess game and upper-stage and off-stage rape of Bianca one of the most brilliantly managed pieces of stagecraft in all of Jacobean drama. Many critics of the play once argued the supposed question of Bianca's 'consent' to the Duke – Schoenbaum, in a notorious phrase, said she 'is able to lose her virtue only because she never really possessed it'[33] – but their encounter is usually read with a different sensibility now. The Duke's cunning is paralleled with Livia's below, in any event, and his language is filled with the rhetoric of masculine power ('Strive not to seek / Thy liberty', 'you shall not out till I'm released', 'I should be sorry the least force should lay / An unkind touch upon thee', 'I can command: / Think upon that') which asserts a familiar pattern of masculine domination/female subjection as well as the more gender-neutral master/subject hierarchical relation. In such a context, Bianca's 'choice' is really non-existent.

Middleton's patterning of sexual violence finally leads to a third rape in the play, one that no other commentator has explored: the murder of Isabella by 'burning treasure' in the masque scene (V.ii).[34] Here Middleton directly equates rape and murder.[35] What actually happens on stage during the masque

---

[32] Dawson, 'Economy of Rape', pp. 303, 304

[33] Schoenbaum, *Middleton's Tragedies*, p. 111. In *Jacobean Tragedy: The Quest for Moral Order* (London, 1962), Irving Ribner refers to Bianca's 'feeble attempts at resistance ... the protests are part of the game' (pp. 144–5). Suzanne Gossett sees the Duke's action as a rape, and groups the play with others of the period which abandon the usual rape-guilt-suicide formula, in ' "Best Men are Molded out of Faults": Marrying the Rapist in Jacobean Drama', *ELR* 14 (1984), 305–27. For a defence of Bianca and an argument for her tragic stature, see Verna Ann Foster, 'The Deed's Creature: The Tragedy of Bianca in *Women Beware Women*', *JEGP* 78 (1979), 508–21.

[34] The nature of this allusion is only glancingly mentioned by Batchelor, 'Pattern', p. 87, and not by Dawson at all.

[35] As Shakespeare does in *Macbeth*, where 'withered Murder' moves 'with Tarquin's ravishing strides' (II.ii.53–6).

scene remains somewhat obscure, as the scene is famously bereft
of stage directions to guide a director through its carnival of
violence. Livia, however, is costumed (in a savage irony) as
'Juno Pronuba, the marriage-goddess' (IV.ii.214) who 'descends'
(V.ii.98 s.d.) from above to choose between two lovers/
shepherds (Hippolito and Guardiano), both in love with a nymph
(Isabella). As she descends, Livia breathes in poisoned incense
prepared by Isabella (in revenge for having lied to her, thereby
permitting her incest with Hippolito). As she recognizes that the
incense 'overcomes' her (V.ii.114), Livia says,

> 'Now for a sign of wealth and golden days,
> Bright-eyed prosperity which all couples love,
> Ay, and makes love, take that!

With no stage direction in O, the verse continues,

> Our brother Jove
> Never denies us of his burning treasure,
> T''express bounty'.
> DUKE   She [Isabella] falls down upon't;
> What's the conceit of that?
> FABRITIO   As over-joyed, belike.
> Too much prosperity overjoys us all,
> And she has her lapful, it seems, my lord.   (V.ii.115–22)

The interpolated stage direction, after Livia's 'take that!', is
'Throws flaming gold upon Isabella, who falls dead'. This stage
direction derives from an annotation, in a seventeenth-century
hand, in the Yale copy of the 1657 octavo.[36]
    Even without the Yale annotation, we can infer the stage action
from Livia's lines. Huston D. Hallahan has noted the traditional
symbolism of such treasure, a double-edged 'sign of wealth that
seems positive but in fact is deadly', linking it to 'the materialism
that dominates the society of the naturalistic plot'.[37] True
enough, but Middleton's allusion to Jove makes clear that Livia's
action concerns more than just a 'sign of wealth', for what is
being represented here is yet another rape – one of the most
famous rapes of antiquity, in fact: Jove 'came / To Danae like a
shoure of golde', according to Ovid.[38] The 'lapful' of 'burning
treasure' in *Women Beware Women* is the image of a violent phallic
penetration. Fabritio's comment even suggests that Livia may

[36] See J. R. Mulryne, 'Annotations in Some Copies of *Two New Plays by Thomas Middleton*, 1657', *Lib* Series 5, 30 (1975), 217–21.
[37] 'The Thematic Juxtaposition of the Representational and the Sensational in Middleton's *Women Beware Women*', *SIcon* 2 (1976), p. 79
[38] *Ovid's Metamorphoses: The Arthur Golding Translation (1567)*, ed. John Frederick Nims (New York, 1965), VI.139

have thrown the gold at Isabella's genitals, as 'lap' had a bawdy as well as a more innocent meaning. As 'Juno', moreover, Livia delivers her 'brother Jove['s]' sexual assault, thus replicating her role as bawd between her own brother and Isabella. Thus Isabella dies – in the physical as well as sexual sense – during a rape. Livia, moreover, is herself killed by a 'precious incense' (V.ii.100) which has been poisoned by Isabella; 'the action', John Potter has noted, 'is a kind of pun on incense/incest; like the incest, the incense is poisoned, and so Livia dies from her own corruption'.[39]

The allusion to Danae carries additional irony when her full story is considered. It was prophesied to her father, King Acrisius of Argos, not only that he would not have a son, but that his daughter would have a son who would kill him. Rather than kill his daughter, the King confined her to an underground chamber, with a single hole open to the sky for light and air. Through this entrance, Jove visited her as a shower of gold, impregnating her with the son, Perseus, who one day indeed killed his grandfather by accident. The story of the father who would confine his daughter lest he die resonates with several elements of Middleton's play, including Bianca's reflection,

> 'Tis not good, in sadness,
> To keep a maid so strict in her young days;
> Restraint breeds wandering thoughts ...
> ...
> I'll nev'r use any girl of mine so strictly;
> Howev'r they're kept, their fortunes find 'em out –
> I see't in me.   (IV.i.30–6)

Bianca's confinement – first by her parents, then by Leantio – also leads to the murder of her 'father', the Duke, a man nearly forty years her senior (he is 'about some fifty-five', which is 'no great age in man', she says, for 'he's then at best / For wisdom and for judgement' [I.iii.92–4]). Isabella's case is the inverse of Bianca's here, as she is publicly shopped by her father, to be married to the foolish Ward.

The images of rape in *Women Beware Women* are surrounded by various other forms of sexual violence and perversion. The Ward represents a vulgar and grotesque phallicism, with his incessant references to sticks, holes and games, embodying the notion of marriage as nothing more than sexual intercourse ('My wife! What can she do?' [II.ii.84]). Yet the Ward's crude desires differ only in degree from Leantio's boastful sexual preening ('I

---

[39] Potter, ' "In Time of Sports" ', p. 380. Potter sees the 'burning treasure' as more directly symbolizing 'Isabella allowing herself to be sold to the Ward ... Her father's answer refers to her lapful of treasure (i.e. the pregnancy that exposes her incest)' (p. 381).

have such luck to flesh. / I never bought a horse but he bore double' [I.iii.51–2]). Leantio's figurative buying of a 'horse' is more literally acted out by the Ward, whose inspection of Isabella's body in III.iii (checking her hair, nose and teeth, peeping under her skirt) is a fantastic instance, at once comic and horrifying, of the male commodification of the female body. Adultery, on the other hand, is a relatively minor sin in the play, and Isabella and Bianca succumb to it for different reasons; the Duke's response to Bianca's protest, 'I have a husband', is a morally hollow glibness: 'That's a single comfort; / Take a friend to him' (II.ii.347–8). The Cardinal's denunciation (IV.i) of his brother's adulterous lust will be neutralized, in the Duke's perverse plan, by the murder of Leantio, and then the Duke's making Bianca 'lawfully mine own, / Without this sin and horror' (IV.i.272–3).

The real 'sin and horror' in *Women Beware Women*, though, is incest. Isabella rejects Hippolito's declaration of love in I.ii, but once deceived by Livia's story of her mother's infidelity in II.i, she gladly embraces Hippolito, adding to it the hypocrisy of marriage to the Ward as a cover-story; mere adultery is evidently more acceptable to her. Hippolito, on the other hand, simply accepts the incest. When Isabella hears the truth in IV.ii, she acknowledges 'sin enough to make a whole world perish' (IV.ii.132) and plots her revenge. It has also been argued that Livia herself harbours incestuous desires for her brother Hippolito, to whom she says, 'Thou keep'st the treasure of that life I love / As dearly as mine own' (II.i.26–7); she provides for his sexual satisfaction as a displacement of her own desire.[40] And Livia's role in the masque is that of Juno, who was both 'sister and wife to Jove' (V.ii.86). But *Women Beware Women* offers us multiple versions of the parent-child incest configuration. As Stephen Wigler has noted, regarding the final sexual pairings in the play, 'the ages of the partners in each liaison differ substantially', and the older partners 'possess parental stature'.[41] Thus the Duke, as we have seen, is fifty-five years old and Bianca not yet sixteen; Middleton, moreover, has increased the age of the historical Duke considerably.[42] Livia – who has already 'buried my two husbands' but 'never mean more to marry' (I.ii.50–1) – is 'nine and thirty' years old (II.ii.157), and Leantio

---

[40] Daniel Dodson first suggested this argument in 'Middleton's Livia', *PQ* 27 (1948), 376–81.

[41] 'Parent and Child: The Pattern of Love in *Women Beware Women*', in '*Accompaninge the players': Essays Celebrating Thomas Middleton, 1580–1980*, ed. Kenneth Friedenreich (New York, 1983), p. 184

[42] The sources do not specifically indicate the Duke's age; historically, he was twenty-three.

perhaps in his early twenties, while Hippolito is the uncle of Isabella, presumably old enough to be her father. The repeated pattern is that the older partner offers peace, comfort, protection, wealth and power to the younger partner.

It is part of Middleton's irony that in each of these cases of real or quasi-incest, something like real love does occur: Livia is sincerely distraught over the death of 'My love's joy' (IV.ii.50), Hippolito embraces Isabella's body and kisses her 'cold lips' (V.ii.134) and Bianca, after kissing the poisoned lips of the Duke, seizes the poisoned cup and drinks. The *Liebestod* motif is very prominent. Yet Middleton's irony extends even further to encompass the means of death for these lovers: Isabella dies from her lapful of burning treasure, Livia is poisoned by incense/incest, Hippolito is shot with poisoned arrows by the Cupids in the masque (he then runs himself upon the guard's weapon) and the Duke drinks from the poisoned chalice. Each of their deaths is sexually inflected, not only a punishment for but also a fulfilment of their sexuality. This bloodbath (and we have not even mentioned Guardiano) has often been attacked as a dramatic failure, but whatever it is, it is surely *not* 'the work of a dramatist who had lost interest in his characters as soon as their emotional development – or deterioration – was complete'.[43] Rather, it seems the work of a dramatist who wanted to drive his characters to the catastrophic completion of their emotional states. The punishment for sexual transgression, it turns out, is sexual punishment.

It is time to step back and consider these interrelated patterns of social and sexual action more generally. *Women Beware Women* represents a striking range of sexual and moral transgression. It is moreover one of the few Jacobean plays which actually feature rape or incest instead of merely threatening them. At the same time, the structure of the play raises central questions of social class and economic position, with Middleton's considerable powers of cultural analysis registering minute social distinctions. The relations between class and sexuality in *Women Beware Women* are too complex to describe simply, but certainly part of their logic is that sexual transgression is expressed as social displacement, and vice versa. The sexual violations in the play may be read under the rubric of the social/political categories of hierarchy and authority: Bianca's rape is more an assertion of the Duke's status than of his desire ('I can command: / Think upon that' [II.ii.362–3]), and adultery is a lesser sin than incest because it does not subvert natural hierarchy, yet still involves

[43] John D. Jump, 'Middleton's Tragedies', in *The Age of Shakespeare*, ed. Boris Ford (Harmondsworth, 1955), p. 360

the strong older/weak younger lover dynamic (Livia tells Fabritio, 'you'd command love – / And so do most old folks that go without it' [I.ii.142–3]). When the Duke decides to eliminate Leantio, he decides to 'flatter' Hippolito with an alleged favour to Livia which he has thought of, 'but nev'r meant to practise – / Because I know her base' (IV. i. 135–7), a social sneer which would certainly have surprised the woman who provided for the Duke in her house. When he informs Hippolito of his sister's new 'bed-fellow', the Duke inflects his account in class terms: Leantio is 'an impudent boaster' who raises 'his glory from her shame . . . [and] wastes her wealth'; worse, the Duke claims, he 'had picked out / A worthy match for her, the great Vincentio, / High in our favour and in all men's thoughts' (IV.i.145–58). Hippolito's reaction to Leantio's name as his sister's sexual partner is all about his class status and youth: 'He's a factor! . . . The poor old widow's son!' (IV.i.162–3).[44] At her death, Bianca realizes that her status at the Duke's palace – indeed, in Florence itself – is artificial and false: 'What make I here? These are all strangers to me, / Not known but by their malice' (V.ii.206–7).[45] The Cardinal's final lines are for the most part conventional piety, but in them Middleton presses, one last time, the play's linking of sexual transgression and social/political hierarchy:

> Sin, what thou art, these ruins show too piteously.
> Two kings on one throne cannot sit together,
> But one must needs down, for his title's wrong;
> So where lust reigns, that prince cannot reign long.   (V.ii.222–5)

'Sin' and 'lust' conspire against sovereignty, but fail because one must down while the other is up, and as for lust, like a would-be royal successor, 'his title's wrong'. So also Leantio argued, at the beginning of the play, when he told his Mother to lower her voice lest Bianca hear her:

> I pray do not you teach her to rebel,
> When she's in a good way to obedience,
> To rise with other women in commotion
> Against their husbands . . .
> . . .

[44] In Webster's *The Duchess of Malfi* (*c.* 1614), Ferdinand has a similar reaction to the news that his sister, the Duchess, has a lover, and he imagines her in the act of sin 'with some strong thigh'd bargeman; / Or one o'th' wood-yard, that can quoit the sledge / Or toss the bar, or else some lovely squire / That carries coals up to her privy lodgings' (II.v.43–6).

[45] R. V. Holdsworth, among others, has noted how ' "strange" and "stranger" are key words' in the play, with twenty-five occurrences, enhancing a 'sense of alienation' felt not only by the characters themselves but by the audience ('*Women Beware Women* and *The Changeling* on the Stage', in *Three Jacobean Revenge Tragedies*, pp. 252–3).

> If you can but rest quiet, she's contented
> With all conditions that my fortunes bring her to:
> To keep close as a wife that loves her husband;
> To go after the rate of my ability,
> Not the licentious swinge of her own will.   (I.i.74–7, 88–92)

Leantio's dream of a love that defies social class and wealth is mocked by his own petty possessiveness, of course, but his vision of disorder here is of the unruly 'will' of the desiring woman; again, the 'licentious' is translated into the social/political, for the assertion of a woman's 'will' would lead her to 'rebel . . . To rise with other women in commotion [i.e. insurrection]'. Their 'obedience' is as devoutly wished for by Leantio as by the Cardinal. Here is the stereotyped spectre of the unruly woman perpetrated by Swetnam and others in the pamphlet wars. The lesson drawn is the misogynist one implied by the play's title, echoed in Bianca's dying words:

> Oh the deadly snares
> That women set for women, without pity
> Either to soul or honour! Learn by me
> To know your foes. In this belief I die:
> Like our own sex, we have no enemy, no enemy!   (V.ii.211–15)

The misogynist position, the play makes clear, is one of hypocrisy. Middleton, it should be emphasized, never excuses the evil his women do in this play. Isabella's plight is terrible, but adultery and incest are equal if not greater horrors; Bianca has no alternative to or escape from the Duke, but her attempted murder of the Cardinal is indefensible and given no rationalization. Livia – a powerful, witty, theatrical woman – turns her considerable gifts to the basest uses more or less on a whim. But what Middleton has done in *Women Beware Women* is to expose the world in which women must live, one in which they are property, and to show how the social structure of this world generates and feeds women's 'rage', 'madness', 'malice' and 'plots'. He stages both their victimization and their self-generating evil; above all, he stages their self-destructiveness, and hence their tragedy.

STAGECRAFT

Two scenes in *Women Beware Women* deserve special attention for their unique interest.

First, there is the celebrated chess scene (II.ii), in which Livia engages the Mother in a game of chess on the stage below while the Duke surprises Bianca on the upper stage. This scene has been universally praised for different reasons. Wholly apart from the elements already mentioned above, for example, Livia's encounter with the Mother is a masterful dialogue reflecting the most minute distinctions of personality and social class; Middleton's brilliance in revealing Livia's ability to manipulate the Mother almost blinds us to her cruelty.

The chess game itself continues the demonstration of Livia's mastery over the Mother, for chess was considered a game appropriate for a higher social class than the Mother inhabits. Middleton has received special praise for the choice of the chess metaphor itself, and for the counterpointing of the two games played above and below. Chess itself is a game which requires extreme aggression within a set of rigid rules and movements – a powerful metaphor for the social dynamics at work among the supposedly friendly enemies of *Women Beware Women*. Middleton has loosely followed the rules and tactics of an actual chess game, moreover, though with far from complete or consistent accuracy. Bianca, whose name means 'white', is 'simplicity' (II.ii.306) or innocence as the white pieces, while Livia is the black queen ('quean' = whore) who defeats white. As the goal of any chess game is checkmating your opponent, so the goal of the Duke's game is sexual mating; the 'death' of the King in chess is simultaneous with the Duke's sexual 'death' offstage. Chess is a game of unusual intellectual violence, then, which Middleton simultaneously produces on the stage. Taylor and Loughrey also point out that 'the world of the chess pieces is hierarchical'[46] – thus the game is an intensely concentrated paradigm of the play's fusion of sexual and social hierarchies.

Chess is, finally, a 'game' – which is, in the play's insistent rhetoric, a sexual term ('game / In a new-married couple' [I.iii.9–10]; 'wise gamesters' [III.iii.107]). *Women Beware Women* is filled with references to games, some of them rustic sports, some upper-class pastimes: Tip-Cat (I.ii.87n.), 'hot-cockles' (I.iii.25n.), 'court-passage' (II.ii.42n.), 'shittlecock' (II.ii.79n.), lawn-bowling (III.i.213n.), fowling (III.iii.17n.), archery (III.iii.19n.), 'stool-ball' (III.iii.87n.) and acrobatics (IV.ii.104n.), among others. What all these games have in common in the play is that they openly, often crudely, figure sexual intercourse. The play's language often becomes extraordinarily dense with obscene innuendo, as a glance at any of the passages listed above will reveal; the very idea of a game is contaminated in the play, as something almost exclusively sexual. Most of the games are initiated by, or won by, men; Livia's mastery at chess is impressive, but it is only over the Mother.

---

[46] See Neil Taylor and Bryan Loughrey, 'Middleton's Chess Strategies in *Women Beware Women*', *SEL* 24 (1984), p. 344.

Middleton would employ chess as a political allegory to much greater effect a few years later in *A Game At Chess* (1624), but though chess is used in only a single scene in *Women*, it is overwhelming in its effect, a theatrical tour de force.

The masque scene (V.ii), by contrast, has been on the receiving end of some extraordinary vituperation even as the play as a whole was being praised. Swinburne termed it 'preposterous beyond extenuation on the score of logical or poetical justice'.[47] J. D. Jump termed it a 'ridiculous holocaust', David Frost saw it as 'arbitrary, an almost farcical tidying up of loose ends', and Schoenbaum felt, simply, 'the last act is a failure, and with it the play collapses'.[48] The most elaborate put-down of the masque scene actually gets at something important about it; for G. R. Hibbard, the play ends 'as a kind of mongrel, the illegitimate offspring of an incongruous union between *The Revenger's Tragedy* and *A Warning for Fair Women*'.[49] The scene's mixture of elements of savage, violent farce and domestic tragedy has struck more recent readers of the play not as a weakness, but as a strength, a mark of Middleton's willingness to experiment; Shand terms the scene 'one of the most daring' finales in Jacobean tragedy.[50] Implicit in many of the criticisms of the scene is a sense of disjunction between dramatic styles felt when the scene begins, an unexplained shift from the supposedly Ibsenesque realism of the first four acts to the final strange mixture which defies a label. Brooke has argued convincingly that, in parallel to its progression up the social scale, the play also moves through 'a progression of dramatic modes ... from comedy through high comedy to tragi-farce'.[51] The amateur play-within-the-play is deliberately awkward, unreal, the genre unable to contain the emotion and violence within it.

The masque scene has always had its defenders. What might be called the 'moral' line of criticism on the play is well represented in Irving Ribner's rigid argument that 'the final scene of mass murder is necessary and proper. It is not to be explained in terms of logical credibility, but rather as the dramatic symbol of the inevitable collapse of a society which by a faulty choice of values inherent in the very nature of humanity has devoted itself to its own destruction'.[52] Batchelor goes so far as to claim that

[47] Quoted in R. V. Holdsworth, ed., *Three Jacobean Revenge Tragedies*, p. 128
[48] Jump, 'Middleton's Tragedies', p. 360; David L. Frost, *The School of Shakespeare* (Cambridge, 1968), p. 69; Schoenbaum, *Middleton's Tragedies*, p. 131
[49] Hibbard, 'The Tragedies of Thomas Middleton', p. 54. Middleton does in fact appear to allude to *A Warning for Fair Women* at II.ii.167–9.
[50] G. B. Shand, 'The Stagecraft of *Women Beware Women*', *RORD* 28 (1985), p. 33
[51] Brooke, *Horrid Laughter*, pp. 104, 108
[52] Ribner, *Jacobean Tragedy*, p. 138

'each death is a moral emblem, a carefully worked model of appropriate retribution seen from the perspective of orthodox Christian dualism', but few have agreed that this perspective is a consistent one, or even 'orthodox'.[53] Many recent defenders of the masque have articulated the links between it and the main play, and especially the logic which drives the death-punishments of each character.[54] Hallahan has further argued that the end of the play conforms to a contemporary 'practice of juxtaposing the unrealistic and extraordinary with the realistic and ordinary'.[55] Jacobean playwrights frequently display a highly self-conscious sense of theatricality, finally, and a play-within-the-play, as here, would hardly have seemed unusual to contemporary audiences.

Middleton's strategy in the masque goes beyond the usual contrasts and parallels of any inner play/outer play dynamic, then, though those links are substantial and important. But Middleton also creates an alternative dramatic model – pastoral, mythological, allegorical – in which women must still beware. The gap between representation and reality seems intentionally large in this other model, but it inscribes, and completes, women's self-destructiveness no less than the rest of the play does.

In terms of more general stagecraft, *Women Beware Women* is exceptional in a number of ways. The play has four major women's parts, for example – perhaps not surprising, given its theme, but certainly a large number compared with most drama of the period. The play as a whole is generously populated with parts large and small, and requires a larger cast than many plays. Middleton also makes extraordinary use of the aside and 'isolation blocking', in Shand's phrase, as a way of enacting alienation: 'the play's tragic figures speak apart almost habitually, even at moments of great intimacy, the effect being that they stand divided from one another, from themselves ... and, at last, from the audience'.[56]

---

[53] Batchelor, 'Pattern', p. 87

[54] See, for example, Hallahan, 'Thematic Juxtaposition'; Inga-Stina Ewbank, ' "These Pretty Devices": A Study of Masques in Plays', in *A Book of Masques* (Cambridge, 1967); Shand, 'Stagecraft'; Holdsworth, '*Women Beware Women* and *The Changeling* on the Stage', in *Three Jacobean Revenge Tragedies*; and Charlotte Spivack, 'Marriage and Masque in Middleton's *Women Beware Women*', CE 42 (1992), 49–55.

[55] 'Thematic Juxtaposition', p. 67

[56] Shand, 'Stagecraft', p. 31

STAGE HISTORY

The stage history of *Women Beware Women* is disappointingly slight.[57] Except for Nathaniel Richards's comment, there is no evidence that the play was professionally performed until the 1960s. The first major production was the 1962 Royal Shakespeare Company production at the New Arts Theatre Club in London, directed by Anthony Page; Nicol Williamson played Leantio. Granada Television filmed a heavily cut version of the play in 1965, with Diana Rigg as Bianca and Clifford Evans as the Duke, and the Traverse Theatre Company performed the play in Edinburgh in 1968. A second Royal Shakespeare production at Stratford in 1969, directed by Terry Hands, was by all accounts highly successful; Richard Pasco played Leantio, Judi Dench Bianca and Brewster Mason the Duke.

Since 1969, the play has received mostly amateur or university stagings. Future stars such as Kevin Kline (as Guardiano, City Center Acting Company, New York, 1972) and Sigourney Weaver (as Mother, Yale School of Drama, 1973) have acted in the play. The film director George Roy Hill set the play in the New Orleans of 1900 in a Yale School of Drama production in 1979. Undoubtedly the most controversial staging of the play was Howard Barker's 1986 adaptation at the Royal Court Theatre in London. Part I of Barker's version was a condensation of the first three and a half acts of Middleton's play; after the intermission, though, the play is entirely by Barker. In Barker's new ending, Sordido becomes a major figure who rapes Bianca on the eve of her wedding; the play now ends with the Duke's cry, 'Don't love! don't love!'.[58] One of the most successful productions of the play was at the Birmingham Repertory Theatre in 1989, directed by John Adams; here, the production was punctuated by 'images of confinement', and the chess scene was played as 'half rape, half seduction, but neither one nor the other'.[59]

Compared with *The Revenger's Tragedy* and *The Changeling*, which have received numerous important productions in the twentieth century and frequent amateur performances, *Women Beware Women* has scarcely been staged at all.

[57] The information in these two paragraphs, except where noted, is from Marilyn Roberts, 'A Preliminary Check-List of Productions of Thomas Middleton's Plays', *RORD* 28 (1985), 37–61.
[58] Thomas Middleton and Howard Barker, *Women Beware Women* (London, 1986), p. 36
[59] Review in *CE* 36 (1989), p. 90

NOTE ON THE TEXT

The earliest known text of *Women Beware Women* is the octavo printed for Humphrey Moseley in 1657: 'TWO NEW PLAYES. / VIZ. More DISSEMBLERS / besides WOMEN. / WOMEN beware / WOMEN. / WRITTEN / By *Tho. Middleton*, Gent.' Mulryne lists twenty-one surviving copies of this octavo, and he has collated twenty of them. No significant variants have been reported. The present text is based on the Huntington Library copy; the Folger, Harvard and Yale copies have also been consulted. I have also profited from consultation of the recent Revels (1975), Cambridge (1978) and Penguin (1988) editions of the play, and of course from Roma Gill's edition of the play (1968) for this series.

Moseley's edition presents an exceptionally clean text. It is likely that the manuscript used in printing was either a scribal transcript of the author's manuscript, or (much less likely) in Middleton's own hand, with perhaps a few annotations by a theatrical book-keeper. For this edition, the spelling has been modernized, some contractions expanded and the punctuation considerably lightened. The play is remarkable for its many asides; they have been marked in the text where there is little doubt of their occurrence. The text presents some difficulties in its erratic intermingling of prose and verse spoken by the Ward and by Sordido; this edition follows, with minor exceptions, the display indicated in the octavo. Thus, there are sometimes prose to verse shifts within a single speech. The justifications for retaining such a display are, first, that the Moseley text is otherwise so meticulous; and second, that the awkward intermixing is a specific rhetorical device to help characterize these low characters. Unless there is strong reason otherwise, the octavo has been followed in such matters as contractions (thus O's 'nev'r' rather than 'ne'er').

Additions or emendations to the text are either indicated in the notes, or indicated by square brackets [ ]. Stage directions present a particular problem here, as they are relatively full but not always clear earlier in the text, and virtually absent during the confusing final scene; all supplementary directions are given in square brackets.

The previous modern editions listed above have done substantial and important work in providing accurate annotation of the text, and I have consulted all of them in preparing this annotation; in addition to adding many of my own notes, I have attempted simply to gloss many words which seem to me now somewhat arcane to the general reader, in the hope of making the play as readable as possible.

FURTHER READING

Barker, Richard H., *Thomas Middleton*, New York, 1958

Batchelor, J. B., 'The Pattern of *Women Beware Women*', YES 2 (1972), 78–88

Brooke, Nicholas, *Horrid Laughter in Jacobean Tragedy*, London, 1979

Cherry, Caroline Lockett, *The Most Unvaluedst Purchase: Women in the Plays of Thomas Middleton*, Salzburg, 1973

Christensen, Ann C. "Settling House in Middleton's *Women Beware Women*." *Comparative Drama* 29 (1995), 493–518

Dawson, Anthony B., '*Women Beware Women* and the Economy of Rape', SEL 27 (1987), 303–20

Eliot, T. S., 'Middleton', in *Selected Essays*, London, 1932

Ellis-Fermor, Una, *Jacobean Drama*, London, 1936

Ewbank, Inga-Stina, 'Realism and Morality in *Women Beware Women*', *Essays and Studies* 22 (1969), 57–70

Friedenreich, Kenneth, ed., '*Accompaninge the players': Essays Celebrating Thomas Middleton, 1580–1980*, New York, 1983

Hallahan, Huston D., 'The Thematic Juxtaposition of the Representational and the Sensational in Middleton's *Women Beware Women*', SIcon 2 (1976), 66–84

Heinemann, Margot, *Puritanism and Theatre: Thomas Middleton and Opposition Drama under the Early Stuarts*, Cambridge, 1980

Holdsworth, R. V., ed., *Three Jacobean Revenge Tragedies: A Casebook*, London, 1990

Lancaster, Marjorie S., 'Middleton's Use of the Upper Stage in *Women Beware Women*', TSE 22 (1977), 69–85

Muir, Kenneth, 'The Role of Livia in *Women Beware Women*', in *Poetry and Drama 1570–1700: Essays in Honour of Harold F. Brooks*, ed. Antony Coleman and Antony Hammond, London, 1981

Mulryne, J. R., *Thomas Middleton*, London, 1979

Parker, R. B., 'Middleton's Experiments with Comedy and Judgement', in *Jacobean Theatre*, ed. J. R. Brown and Bernard A. Harris, Stratford-upon-Avon, 1960

Potter, John, ' "In Time of Sports": Masques and Masking in Middleton's *Women Beware Women*', PLL 18 (1982), 368–83

Shand, G. B. 'The Stagecraft of *Women Beware Women*', RORD 28 (1985), 29–36

Taylor, Neil, and Loughrey, Bryan, 'Middleton's Chess Strategies in *Women Beware Women*,' SEL 24 (1984), 341–54

Thomson, Leslie, ' "Enter Above": The Staging of *Women Beware Women*', *SEL* 26 (1986), 331–43

Tricomi, Albert H., *Anticourt Drama in England 1603–1642*, Charlottesville, 1989

(Opposite) Title page from the 1657 edition of *Two New Plays* reproduced by courtesy of the British Library.

WOMEN
BEWARE
WOMEN.

A
TRAGEDY,
BY
Tho. Middleton, Gent.

LONDON:

Printed for *Humphrey Moseley*, 1657.

TO THE READER

When these amongst others of Mr. Thomas Middleton's
excellent poems came to my hands, I was not a little
confident but that his name would prove as great an induce-
ment for thee to read, as me to print them, since those
issues of his brain that have already seen the sun have by   5
their worth gained themselves a free entertainment
amongst all that are ingenious; and I am most certain that
these will no way lessen his reputation, nor hinder his
admission to any noble and recreative spirits. All that I
require at thy hands is to continue the author in his deserved   10
esteem, and to accept of my endeavours which have ever
been to please thee.

Farewell

---

1 *these Women Beware Women* (*c.* 1621) was printed together with *More Dissemblers
Besides Women* (*c.* 1615–19) as *Two New Playes* by Humphrey Moseley in 1657.
Moseley also published *No Wit, No Help Like a Woman's* (*c.* 1611) in a separate
octavo in 1657.

2

Upon The Tragedy of
My Familiar Acquaintance,
Thomas Middleton

Women beware Women: 'tis a true text
Never to be forgot. Drabs of state vexed
Have plots, poisons, mischiefs that seldom miss
To murder virtue with a venom kiss.
Witness this worthy tragedy, expressed   5
By him that well deserved among the best
Of poets in his time. He knew the rage,
Madness of women crossed; and for the stage
Fitted their humours, hell-bred malice, strife
Acted in state, presented to the life.   10
I that have seen't can say, having just cause,
Never came tragedy off with more applause.

Nathaniel Richards

---

2 *Drabs of state* whores of great men
10 *in state* with great pomp and ceremony
13 A dramatist and poet, known especially for his play *The Tragedy of Messalina* (pr. 1640), Richards may have been responsible for delivering a copy of Middleton's play to the printer, Moseley. Richards could have seen the play at any time between *c.* 1621 and 1642, the closing of the theatres; no other record of performance exists.

DRAMATIS PERSONAE

DUKE OF FLORENCE
LORD CARDINAL, brother to the DUKE
TWO CARDINALS more
A LORD
FABRITIO, father to ISABELLA [and brother to LIVIA and 5
    HIPPOLITO]
HIPPOLITO, brother to FABRITIO [and LIVIA, uncle to
    ISABELLA]
GUARDIANO, uncle to the foolish WARD
THE WARD, a rich young heir 10
LEANTIO, a factor, husband to BIANCA
SORDIDO, the WARD's man

LIVIA, sister to FABRITIO [and HIPPOLITO, aunt to ISABELLA]
ISABELLA, niece to LIVIA [and HIPPOLITO, daughter of
    FABRITIO] 15
BIANCA, LEANTIO's wife
WIDOW, his [LEANTIO's] mother

STATES of FLORENCE
CITIZENS
A 'PRENTICE 20
BOYS
MESSENGER
SERVANTS
[Two LADIES, LORDS, PAGES, GUARD]
[Figures in the Masque: HYMEN, GANYMEDE, HEBE, 25
    NYMPHS, CUPIDS]

The Scene:
FLORENCE

---

11 *factor* commercial agent
   BIANCA ed. (Brancha O) The octavo spells her name 'Brancha' throughout – a
misreading of Middleton's 'e' ('Beancha') or, less likely, his 'i' ('Biancha').
Middleton's source, Malespini's *Ducento Novelle*, spells the name 'Bianca'; in
several places in the play, moreover, the metre requires a tri-syllabic pro-
nunciation – hence, 'Bianca'.
18 *STATES* nobility
20 *A 'PRENTICE* an apprentice

4

WOMEN BEWARE WOMEN

Act I, Scene i

Enter LEANTIO *with* BIANCA *and* MOTHER
[Bianca stands apart]

MOTHER
Thy sight was never yet more precious to me;
Welcome with all the affection of a mother,
That comfort can express from natural love.
Since thy birth-joy – a mother's chiefest gladness,
After sh'as undergone her curse of sorrows –   5
Thou wast not more dear to me than this hour
Presents thee to my heart. Welcome again.
LEANTIO
[Aside] 'Las poor affectionate soul, how her joys speak
    to me!
I have observed it often, and I know it is
The fortune commonly of knavish children   10
To have the loving'st mothers.
MOTHER   What's this gentlewoman?
LEANTIO
Oh you have named the most unvalued'st purchase
That youth of man had ever knowledge of.
As often as I look upon that treasure
And know it to be mine – there lies the blessing –   15
It joys me that I ever was ordained
To have a being, and to live 'mongst men;
Which is a fearful living, and a poor one,
Let a man truly think on't.
To have the toil and griefs of fourscore years   20
Put up in a white sheet, tied with two knots –
Methinks it should strike earthquakes in adulterers,
When ev'n the very sheets they commit sin in

3 *express* distil, press out
5 *curse of sorrows* pain of childbirth (cf. Genesis 3:16)
12 *unvalued'st* invaluable, inestimable
12–14 *purchase . . . treasure* The expression of personal relations in the language of
    commerce, discussed in the Introduction, begins here.
21 *white sheet . . . two knots* funeral shroud, fastened by knot at head and feet

5

May prove, for aught they know, all their last garments.
Oh what a mark were there for women then!   25
But beauty able to content a conqueror,
Whom earth could scarce content, keeps me in compass;
I find no wish in me bent sinfully
To this man's sister, or to that man's wife:
In love's name let 'em keep their honesties,   30
And cleave to their own husbands, 'tis their duties.
Now when I go to church, I can pray handsomely;
Not come like gallants only to see faces,
As if lust went to market still on Sundays.
I must confess I am guilty of one sin, Mother,   35
More than I brought into the world with me,
But that I glory in: 'tis theft, but noble
As ever greatness yet shot up withal.

MOTHER
How's that?

LEANTIO   Never to be repented, Mother,
Though sin be death; I had died, if I had not sinned,   40
And here's my masterpiece: do you now behold her!
Look on her well, she's mine, look on her better –
Now say, if 't be not the best piece of theft
That ever was committed; and I have my pardon for't:
'Tis sealed from Heaven by marriage.

MOTHER   Married to her!   45

LEANTIO
You must keep counsel, Mother, I am undone else;
If it be known, I have lost her; do but think now
What that loss is – life's but a trifle to't.
From Venice, her consent and I have brought her
From parents great in wealth, more now in rage;   50
But let storms spend their furies. Now we have got
A shelter o'er our quiet innocent loves,
We are contented. Little money sh'as brought me.

25 *mark* example
26 *conqueror* Alexander the Great is said to have wept because there were no more
   worlds to conquer.
27 *in compass* within limits
30 *honesties* chastities
32–4 *Now . . . Sundays* Many writers of the time complained that church-going had
   become merely a social event.
35–6 *sin . . . with me* original sin
37–8 *'tis theft . . . withal* a theft as noble as any that ever helped a great man rise in
   the world
40 *sin be death* allusion to Romans 6:23: 'the wages of sin is death'
46 *keep counsel* keep it secret

View but her face, you may see all her dowry,
Save that which lies locked up in hidden virtues,   55
Like jewels kept in cabinets.
MOTHER   Y'are to blame,
If your obedience will give way to a check,
To wrong such a perfection.
LEANTIO   How?
MOTHER   Such a creature,
To draw her from her fortune, which no doubt,
At the full time, might have proved rich and noble: 60
You know not what you have done. My life can give you
But little helps, and my death lesser hopes;
And hitherto your own means has but made shift
To keep you single, and that hardly too.
What ableness have you to do her right, then,   65
In maintenance fitting her birth and virtues?
Which ev'ry woman of necessity looks for,
And most to go above it, not confined
By their conditions, virtues, bloods, or births,
But flowing to affections, wills, and humours.   70
LEANTIO

Speak low, sweet Mother; you are able to spoil as many
As come within the hearing; if it be not
Your fortune to mar all, I have much marvel.
I pray do not you teach her to rebel,
When she's in a good way to obedience,   75
To rise with other women in commotion
Against their husbands, for six gowns a year,
And so maintain their cause, when they're once up,
In all things else that require cost enough.
They are all of 'em a kind of spirits soon raised,   80
But not so soon laid, Mother. As for example,

---

56 *to blame* ed. (too blame O). Middleton frequently uses 'blame' as an adjective
   and 'to' as the adverb 'too', i.e. too blameworthy; this edition modernizes the
   seven occurrences in the play to the more familiar 'to blame'.
57 *check* a rebuke, but also a term in chess, anticipating the chess game in II.ii
63 *but made shift* barely managed
64 *keep you single* maintain you as a bachelor
   hardly in hard circumstances; with difficulty
69–70 *conditions ... humours* i.e. most women seek to go beyond 'necessity' – the
   social and biological limitations of their births – to satisfy the less stable demands
   of desire ('affections' = passions; 'wills' = sexual desire; 'humours' = whims
   of personality)
76 *commotion* disorder, insurrection
80–1 *spirits ... laid* like demons or ghosts called up ('raised') or sent down ('laid');
   but also sexual connotations of arousal and orgasm, as in ll. 82–3

A woman's belly is got up in a trice –
A simple charge ere it be laid down again;
So ever in all their quarrels, and their courses.
And I'm a proud man, I hear nothing of 'em,   85
They're very still, I thank my happiness,
And sound asleep; pray let not your tongue wake 'em.
If you can but rest quiet, she's contented
With all conditions that my fortunes bring her to:
To keep close as a wife that loves her husband;   90
To go after the rate of my ability,
Not the licentious swinge of her own will,
Like some of her old schoolfellows. She intends
To take out other works in a new sampler,
And frame the fashion of an honest love,   95
Which knows no wants but, mocking poverty,
Brings forth more children, to make rich men wonder
At divine Providence, that feeds mouths of infants,
And sends them none to feed, but stuffs their rooms
With fruitful bags, their beds with barren wombs.   100
Good Mother, make not you things worse than they are,
Out of your too much openness – pray take heed on't –
Nor imitate the envy of old people,
That strive to mar good sport, because they are perfect.
I would have you more pitiful to youth,   105
Especially to your own flesh and blood.
I'll prove an excellent husband, here's my hand;
Lay in provision, follow my business roundly,
And make you a grandmother in forty weeks.
Go, pray salute her, bid her welcome cheerfully.   110
MOTHER
Gentlewoman, thus much is a debt of courtesy
Which fashionable strangers pay each other
At a kind meeting [*Kisses* BIANCA]; then there's more
    than one,

83 *simple charge* ironic: actually, a difficult or expensive business
90 *keep close* live a secluded life
91–2 *rate ... will* i.e. to live according to my means, rather than the unchecked inclinations of her own desires; but also with suggestion of her loose sexual desires
92 *swinge* freedom of action; impulse
94 *take ... sampler* i.e. unlike other women, she will copy other forms (of behaviour) in a new model. The metaphor of embroidery continues in 'frame', l. 95.
100 *bags* money bags
104 *perfect* completed, contented
108 *business roundly* 'Business' frequently has a sexual connotation in the play; 'roundly' = energetically. The phrase anticipates the wife's pregnancy, referred to in l. 109.

Due to the knowledge I have of your nearness.
I am bold to come again, [*Kisses her again*] and now
  salute you   115
By th'name of daughter, which may challenge more
Than ordinary respect. [*Kisses her again*]
LEANTIO [*Aside*]   Why, this is well now,
And I think few mothers of threescore will mend it.
MOTHER
What I can bid you welcome to, is mean;
But make it all your own; we are full of wants,   120
And cannot welcome worth.
LEANTIO [*Aside*]   Now this is scurvy,
And spake as if a woman lacked her teeth.
These old folks talk of nothing but defects,
Because they grow so full of 'em themselves.
BIANCA
Kind Mother, there is nothing can be wanting   125
To her that does enjoy all her desires.
Heaven send a quiet peace with this man's love,
And I am as rich as virtue can be poor;
Which were enough after the rate of mind,
To erect temples for content placed here.   130
I have forsook friends, fortunes, and my country,
And hourly I rejoice in't. Here's my friends,
And few is the good number. [*To* LEANTIO] Thy
  successes,
Howe'er they look, I will still name my fortunes;
Hopeful or spiteful, they shall all be welcome.   135
Who invites many guests has of all sorts,
As he that traffics much drinks of all fortunes;
Yet they must all be welcome, and used well.
I'll call this place the place of my birth now,
And rightly too, for here my love was born,   140
And that's the birthday of a woman's joys.
You have not bid me welcome since I came.
LEANTIO
That I did questionless.
BIANCA   No sure, how was't?
I have quite forgot it.
LEANTIO [*Kisses her*]   Thus.

118 *mend it* do it better
120 *wants* deficiencies
121 *scurvy* irritating; also, the disease
122 *lacked her teeth* one symptom of scurvy
129 i.e. as measured by the standard of the contented mind
137 *traffics* trades

BIANCA   Oh sir, 'tis true,
Now I remember well. I have done thee wrong,   145
Pray tak't again, sir. [*Kisses him*]
LEANTIO   How many of these wrongs
Could I put up in an hour, and turn up the glass
For twice as many more!
MOTHER
Will't please you to walk in, daughter?
BIANCA   Thanks, sweet
    Mother;
The voice of her that bare me, is not more pleasing.   150
                    Exeunt [MOTHER *and* BIANCA]
LEANTIO
Though my own care and my rich master's trust
Lay their commands both on my factorship,
This day and night I'll know no other business
But her and her dear welcome. 'Tis a bitterness
To think upon tomorrow, that I must leave her   155
Still to the sweet hopes of the week's end.
That pleasure should be so restrained and curbed
After the course of a rich workmaster,
That never pays till Saturday night!
Marry, it comes together in a round sum then,   160
And does more good, you'll say. Oh fair-eyed Florence!
Didst thou but know what a most matchless jewel
Thou now art mistress of, a pride would take thee,
Able to shoot destruction through the bloods
Of all thy youthful sons! But 'tis great policy   165
To keep choice treasures in obscurest places:
Should we show thieves our wealth, 'twould make 'em
    bolder.
Temptation is a devil will not stick
To fasten upon a saint; take heed of that.
The jewel is cased up from all men's eyes;   170
Who could imagine now a gem were kept,
Of that great value, under this plain roof?
But how in times of absence? What assurance
Of this restraint then? Yes, yes – there's one with her.
Old mothers know the world; and such as these,   175
When sons lock chests, are good to look to keys.   *Exit*

147 *turn up the glass* turn over an hour-glass
152 *factorship* Leantio is a clerk or agent for a merchant.
158 *After* dependent on
163 *pride* a sense of pride; but also with strong sexual overtone
165 *policy* cunning
168 *stick* hesitate

Act I, Scene ii

Enter GUARDIANO, FABRITIO, *and* LIVIA
[*and* SERVANT]

GUARDIANO
What, has your daughter seen him yet? Know you that?
FABRITIO
No matter, she shall love him.
GUARDIANO   Nay, let's have fair play,
He has been now my ward some fifteen year,
And 'tis my purpose – as time calls upon me –
By custom seconded, and such moral virtues,   5
To tender him a wife. Now, sir, this wife
I'd fain elect out of a daughter of yours.
You see my meaning's fair; if now this daughter
So tendered – let me come to your own phrase, sir –
Should offer to refuse him, I were hanselled.   10
[*Aside*] Thus am I fain to calculate all my words
For the meridian of a foolish old man,
To take his understanding! [*To him*] What do you
    answer, sir?
FABRITIO
I say still she shall love him.
GUARDIANO   Yet again?
And shall she have no reason for this love?   15
FABRITIO
Why, do you think that women love with reason?
GUARDIANO
[*Aside*] I perceive fools are not at all hours foolish,
No more than wise men wise.
FABRITIO   I had a wife,
She ran mad for me; she had no reason for't,

---

3 *ward* The guardian of a ward would want to marry off his charge before he
reached the age of majority (21), in order to secure a payment from the father of
the bride or, if his ward refused the match, a fine from the estate. This relationship
led to extensive corruption on the part of guardians at the time. If the bride
refused the match, however, no fine could be levied.
4 *as time calls upon me* The Ward is 'almost twenty' (l. 78), hence almost at the age
of majority.
10 *hanselled* A 'hansel' is a gift given at the beginning of the New Year or a new
venture; Guardiano's allusion is thus ironic – i.e. he would be left with little.
12 *meridian* point of highest development (in this case, intellectual)
13 *take* measure; catch
17 *fools . . . foolish* proverbial

For aught I could perceive. What think you,   20
Lady sister?
GUARDIANO [*Aside*] 'Twas a fit match that,
Being both out of their wits. [*To him*] A loving wife, it
    seemed,
She strove to come as near you as she could.
FABRITIO
And if her daughter prove not mad for love too,
She takes not after her; nor after me,   25
If she prefer reason before my pleasure.
[*To* LIVIA] You're an experienced widow, lady sister,
I pray let your opinion come amongst us.
LIVIA
I must offend you then, if truth will do't,
And take my niece's part, and call't injustice   30
To force her love to one she never saw.
Maids should both see, and like – all little enough;
If they love truly after that, 'tis well.
Counting the time, she takes one man till death,
That's a hard task, I tell you; but one may   35
Enquire at three years' end amongst young wives,
And mark how the game goes.
FABRITIO   Why, is not man
Tied to the same observance, lady sister,
And in one woman?
LIVIA   'Tis enough for him;
Besides, he tastes of many sundry dishes   40
That we poor wretches never lay our lips to –
As obedience, forsooth, subjection, duty, and such
    kickshaws,
All of our making, but served in to them.
And if we lick a finger then sometimes
We are not to blame: your best cooks use it.   45
FABRITIO
Th'art a sweet lady, sister, and a witty –

20–1 *you, / Lady* ed. (you Lady O)
30–3 *injustice . . . well* Jacobean discourse frequently debated the legal and moral
    rights of a father to marry off his daughter to whomever he chose; technically,
    the daughter had to consent to the marriage. Plays such as George Wilkins's *The
    Miseries of Enforced Marriage* (1607) dramatized real-life cases.
34 *Counting* considering
37 *game* with sexual connotation
42 *kickshaws* fancy dishes (i.e. trifles)
44–5 *lick a finger . . . best cooks* i.e. women should have some of the same rights to
    'taste' as men. Livia's egalitarian point, however, is made through an obscene
    sexual metaphor which foreshadows the sexual transgressions to come.

LIVIA

A witty! Oh the bud of commendation
Fit for a girl of sixteen! I am blown, man,
I should be wise by this time – and for instance,
I have buried my two husbands in good fashion,   50
And never mean more to marry.

GUARDIANO   No, why so, lady?

LIVIA

Because the third shall never bury me.
I think I am more than witty; how think you, sir?

FABRITIO

I have paid often fees to a counsellor
Has had a weaker brain.

LIVIA   Then I must tell you,   55
Your money was soon parted.

GUARDIANO [*To* FABRITIO]   Light her now, brother!

LIVIA

Where is my niece? Let her be sent for straight.
                                        [*Exit* SERVANT]
If you have any hope 'twill prove a wedding,
'Tis fit i'faith she should have one sight of him,
And stop upon't, and not be joined in haste,   60
As if they went to stock a new-found land.

FABRITIO

Look out her uncle, and y'are sure of her,
Those two are nev'r asunder: they've been heard
In argument at midnight, moonshine nights
Are noondays with them; they walk out their sleeps,   65
Or rather at those hours appear like those
That walk in 'em, for so they did to me.
Look you, I told you truth; they're like a chain,

---

48 *blown* fully blossomed, no longer a 'bud' (l. 47)
56 *Your . . . parted* 'A fool and his money are soon parted' (Tilley, F 452).
   Light . . . brother! O's line has seemed obscure to many editors, leading to such
   emendations as 'like enow', with 'Brother' given to Livia, and 'Plight her now',
   again giving 'Brother' to Livia. Gill suggests, reasonably, that 'perhaps Guardiano
   is inciting Fabritio to answer Livia, to bring her down, now she is in full, witty
   flight?' The term 'brother' could be used very loosely.
61 *stock a new-found land* Middleton refers to the hastily-arranged marriages – in
   some cases, the couples had not previously met – designed to populate one of
   the New World colonies, probably Virginia: 'Take deliberation, sir, never choose
   a wife as if you were going to Virginia' (*The Roaring Girl* II.ii.66–7).
65 *walk . . . sleeps* walk together rather than sleep

Draw but one link, all follows.

Enter HIPPOLITO *and* ISABELLA *the niece*

GUARDIANO   Oh affinity,
What piece of excellent workmanship art thou!   70
'Tis work clean wrought, for there's no lust, but love
    in't,
And that abundantly; when in stranger things
There is no love at all, but what lust brings.

FABRITIO
[*To* ISABELLA] On with your mask, for 'tis your part to
    see now,
And not be seen. Go to, make use of your time;   75
See what you mean to like; nay, and I charge you,
Like what you see. Do you hear me? There's no
    dallying.
The gentleman's almost twenty, and 'tis time
He were getting lawful heirs, and you a-breeding on
    'em.

ISABELLA
Good father!
FABRITIO   Tell not me of tongues and rumours!   80
You'll say the gentleman is somewhat simple –
The better for a husband, were you wise,
For those that marry fools, live ladies' lives.
On with the mask, I'll hear no more, he's rich;
The fool's hid under bushels. [ISABELLA *puts on mask*]   85
LIVIA   Not so hid neither,
But here's a foul great piece of him, methinks;
What will he be, when he comes altogether?

Enter the WARD *with a trap-stick, and* SORDIDO *his man*

WARD
Beat him?
I beat him out o'th'field with his own cat-stick,
. Yet gave him the first hand.
SORDIDO   Oh strange!
WARD   I did it,   90

71 *clean* competent; morally pure
72 *stranger things* men and women not related, hence strangers
80 *tongues* gossip   85 *bushels* large quantities (of money, in his case)
87 s.d. *trap-stick* also 'cat-stick' (l. 89). A cat-stick was used in the country game of
    Tip-Cat (or Cat-and-Trap) to strike a wooden 'cat' (a short piece of wood tapered
    outward at both ends) so that it flies into the air, where it can be struck again.
90 *first hand* the first strike in the game

Then he set jacks on me.

SORDIDO   What, my lady's tailor?

WARD

Ay, and I beat him too.

SORDIDO   Nay, that's no wonder,
He's used to beating.

WARD   Nay, I tickled him
When I came once to my tippings.

SORDIDO   Now you talk on 'em,
There was a poulterer's wife made a great complaint of   95
you last night to your guardianer, that you struck a bump
in her child's head, as big as an egg.

WARD

An egg may prove a chicken then, in time; the poulterer's
wife will get by't. When I am in game, I am furious;
came my mother's eyes in my way, I would not lose a fair   100
end. No, were she alive, but with one tooth in her head,
I should venture the striking out of that. I think of nobody
when I am in play, I am so earnest. Coads-me, my
guardianer! Prithee lay up my cat and cat-stick safe.

SORDIDO

Where, sir, i'th'chimney-corner?

WARD   Chimney-corner!   105

SORDIDO

Yes, sir, your cats are always safe i'th'chimney-corner,
Unless they burn their coats.

WARD   Marry, that I am afraid on.

SORDIDO

Why, then I will bestow your cat i'th'gutter,
And there she's safe, I am sure.

WARD   If I but live
To keep a house, I'll make thee a great man,   110

---

91 *jacks* common fellows
  tailor Tailors were proverbially cowards (and thieves).
93 *beating* used to being beaten; used to 'beaten' or embroidered cloth
94 *tippings* presumably a term in the Tip-Cat game
95–104 A prose passage suddenly intrudes into the verse – a common occurrence
  in this play. The alternation of prose and verse helps characterize the Ward
  throughout, a country bumpkin whose efforts at higher social discourse continually collapse back into such colloquial prose.
96 *guardianer* guardian
99 *get* gain   *in game* playing Tip-Cat; having sex
100–1 *fair end* good result
103 *Coads-me* i.e. 'egad' – a mild oath
106–7 *cats . . . chimney . . . burn* sexual innuendo: 'cats' = whores; 'chimney' = female
  genitals; 'burn' = symptom of venereal disease

If meat and drink can do't. I can stoop gallantly,
And pitch out when I list; I'm dog at a hole.
I mar'l my guardianer does not seek a wife for me;
I protest I'll have a bout with the maids else,
Or contract my self at midnight to the larder-woman,   115
In presence of a fool or a sack-posset.

GUARDIANO
 Ward!

WARD   I feel myself after any exercise
 Horribly prone. Let me but ride, I'm lusty,
 A cock-horse straight, i'faith.

GUARDIANO   Why, ward, I say!

WARD
 I'll forswear eating eggs in moonshine nights;   120
 There's nev'r a one I eat, but turns into a cock
 In four and twenty hours; if my hot blood
 Be not took down in time, sure 'twill crow shortly.

GUARDIANO
 Do you hear, sir? Follow me, I must new school you.

WARD   ◑
 School me? I scorn that now, I am past schooling.   125
 I am not so base to learn to write and read;
 I was born to better fortunes in my cradle.
                     Exit [WARD, GUARDIANO, *and* SORDIDO]

FABRITIO
 [*To* ISABELLA] How do you like him, girl? This is your
   husband.
 Like him or like him not, wench, you shall have him,

111–12 *stoop gallantly . . . pitch out . . . dog at a hole* All three are terms from a game,
 perhaps Tip-Cat, but all are also sexual puns: 'stoop gallantly', according to
 Mulryne, alludes to 'stoop-gallant', a term for venereal disease; 'pitch out' =
 ejaculation; 'hole' = female genitals.

113 *mar'l* abbreviation for 'marvel'

116 *fool* A verbal 'contract' for marriage was enacted if the proper words of declaration
 were spoken in the presence of a witness; but since this witness would be a 'fool',
 the contract would not be binding. Touchstone seeks a similarly flawed contract
 when he engages Sir Oliver Martext to marry him in *As You Like It* (III.ii).
 fool . . . sack-posset 'Fool' is a dish of fruit mixed with cream, a kind of trifle; 'sack-
 posset' was a drink made with sack, sugar, eggs and spices.

118 *prone* i.e. to lechery

118–19 *ride . . . cock-horse* a child's hobby-horse; also with strong sexual connotation
 of a loose woman

120 *eggs . . . nights* Eggs were thought to be an aphrodisiac; 'moonshine nights' were
 traditionally times of sexual festivity and release. Mulryne also suggests 'eggs-in-
 moonshine', a dish resembling poached eggs.

121–3 *cock . . . took down . . . crow* i.e. the cock will crow, but also the Ward's phallus
 will ejaculate ('crow') if it is not detumesced ('took down')

And you shall love him.   130

LIVIA

Oh soft there, brother! Though you be a Justice,
Your warrant cannot be served out of your liberty.
You may compel, out of the power of father,
Things merely harsh to a maid's flesh and blood,
But when you come to love, there the soil alters;   135
Y'are in another country, where your laws
Are no more set by, than the cacklings of geese
In Rome's great Capitol.

FABRITIO   Marry him she shall, then,
Let her agree upon love afterwards.   *Exit*

LIVIA

You speak now, brother, like an honest mortal   140
That walks upon th'earth with a staff;
You were up i'th'clouds before. You'd command love –
And so do most old folks that go without it.
[*To* HIPPOLITO] My best and dearest brother, I could
    dwell here;
There is not such another seat on earth,   145
Where all good parts better express themselves.

HIPPOLITO

You'll make me blush anon.

LIVIA

'Tis but like saying grace before a feast, then,
And that's most comely; thou art all a feast,
And she that has thee, a most happy guest.   150
Prithee cheer up thy niece with special counsel.   [*Exit*]

HIPPOLITO

[*Aside*] I would 'twere fit to speak to her what I would;
    but
'Twas not a thing ordained, Heaven has forbid it;
And 'tis most meet that I should rather perish
Than the decree divine receive least blemish.   155
Feed inward, you my sorrows, make no noise,
Consume me silent, let me be stark dead
Ere the world know I'm sick. You see my honesty;

---

131 *Justice* a Justice of the Peace
132 *liberty* area of his legal jurisdiction
137–8 *geese ... Capitol* Juno's sacred geese were kept on the Capitoline Hill. Their
    cackling once awoke the Romans to a surprise attack by the Gauls, but Livia's
    analogy seems to dismiss their effectiveness here.
146 *parts* qualities of mind and body
151 *thy* ed. (that O)
158 *You* presumably a reference to 'you my sorrows' (l. 156)

If you befriend me, so.
ISABELLA [*Aside*]   Marry a fool!
Can there be greater misery to a woman   160
That means to keep her days true to her husband,
And know no other man! So virtue wills it.
Why, how can I obey and honour him,
But I must needs commit idolatry?
A fool is but the image of a man,   165
And that but ill made neither. Oh the heart-breakings
Of miserable maids, where love's enforced!
The best condition is but bad enough:
When women have their choices, commonly
They do but buy their thraldoms, and bring great
   portions   170
To men to keep 'em in subjection –
As if a fearful prisoner should bribe
The keeper to be good to him, yet lies in still,
And glad of a good usage, a good look
Sometimes. By'r Lady, no misery surmounts a
   woman's!   175
Men buy their slaves, but women buy their masters;
Yet honesty and love makes all this happy
And, next to angels', the most blest estate.
That Providence, that has made ev'ry poison
Good for some use, and sets four warring elements   180
At peace in man, can make a harmony
In things that are most strange to human reason.
Oh but this marriage! [*To him*] What, are you sad too,
   uncle?
'Faith, then there's a whole household down together.
Where shall I go to seek my comfort now   185
When my best friend's distressed? What is't afflicts you,
   sir?
HIPPOLITO
'Faith, nothing but one grief that will not leave me,

164–5 *idolatry . . . image* She doubly commits idolatry, because a fool is only an 'image' of a man, and man is the image of God.
170 *portions* marriage dowries
175 *Sometimes. By'r* ed. (Sometimes by'r O)   178 *estate* condition
180 *four warring elements* Earth, air, fire and water, combined in equal portions, form an ideal balance of nature or psychological state. Perhaps an echo of *I Tamburlaine*: 'Nature that framed us of four elements / Warring within our breasts for regiment, / Doth teach us all to have aspiring minds' (II.vii.18–20). In saying that 'Providence' 'sets four warring elements / At peace', Isabella is inverting Tamburlaine's much different view that 'Nature' sets these elements at war; her naivety will soon vanish.

And now 'tis welcome; ev'ry man has something
To bring him to his end, and this will serve,
Joined with your father's cruelty to you –   190
That helps it forward.

ISABELLA   Oh be cheered, sweet uncle!
How long has't been upon you? I nev'r spied it;
What a dull sight have I! How long, I pray, sir?

HIPPOLITO
Since I first saw you, niece, and left Bologna.

ISABELLA
And could you deal so unkindly with my heart,   195
To keep it up so long hid from my pity?
Alas, how shall I trust your love hereafter?
Have we passed through so many arguments,
And missed of that still, the most needful one?
Walked out whole nights together in discourses,   200
And the main point forgot? We are to blame both;
This is an obstinate, wilful forgetfulness,
And faulty on both parts. Let's lose no time now.
Begin, good uncle, you that feel't; what is it?

HIPPOLITO
You of all creatures, niece, must never hear on't,   205
'Tis not a thing ordained for you to know.

ISABELLA
Not I, sir! All my joys that word cuts off;
You made profession once you loved me best –
'Twas but profession!

HIPPOLITO   Yes, I do't too truly,
And fear I shall be chid for't. Know the worst, then: 210
I love thee dearlier than an uncle can.

ISABELLA
Why, so you ever said, and I believed it.

HIPPOLITO
[Aside] So simple is the goodness of her thoughts,
They understand not yet th'unhallowed language
Of a near sinner. I must yet be forced –   215
Though blushes be my venture – to come nearer.
[To her] As a man loves his wife, so love I thee.

ISABELLA   What's
    that?

196 *keep* shut
198 *arguments* topics, discussions
216 *nearer* become more explicit; get even closer

Methought I heard ill news come toward me,
Which commonly we understand too soon,
Than over-quick at hearing. I'll prevent it,   220
Though my joys fare the harder. Welcome it?
It shall nev'r come so near mine ear again.
Farewell all friendly solaces and discourses,
I'll learn to live without ye, for your dangers
Are greater than your comforts. What's become   225
Of truth in love, if such we cannot trust,
When blood that should be love is mixed with lust?
                                                                    Exit

HIPPOLITO
The worst can be but death, and let it come;
He that lives joyless, ev'ry day's his doom.   *Exit*

Act I, Scene iii

Enter LEANTIO *alone*

LEANTIO
Methinks I'm ev'n as dull now at departure
As men observe great gallants the next day
After a revels; you shall see 'em look
Much of my fashion, if you mark 'em well.
'Tis ev'n a second Hell to part from pleasure   5
When man has got a smack on't. As many holidays
Coming together makes your poor heads idle
A great while after, and are said to stick
Fast in their fingers' ends, ev'n so does game

218–25 Somewhat obscure passage. The first hint of bad news, she implies, will be
  understood immediately, even sooner than merely hearing it; rather than welcome
  it, she will forestall ever hearing it by forswearing all discourse.
220 *Than* ed. (Then O). This seems a comparative, but O may also be correct, as
  Holdsworth (p. 89) notes.
  prevent anticipate
227 *blood* Isabella means 'natural relation', but the word also suggests, contrary to
  her intention, 'sexual desire'. The word 'blood' appears frequently in the play;
  its meaning may range from 'birth' or 'natural relations', to 'inclination', 'arousal',
  'desire' and 'sexual appetite'. Several quite different meanings may be invoked
  simultaneously, as here.
6 *smack* taste
8–9 *stick ... ends* Frost suggests their 'aching head in hand', but it seems more
  likely to refer to a physical inability (parallel to the intellectual one, 'poor heads
  idle') after 'many holidays'.
9 *game* sexual pleasure

In a new-married couple for the time;   10
It spoils all thrift, and indeed lies a-bed
To invent all the new ways for great expenses.

[*Enter*] BIANCA *and* MOTHER *above*

See, and she be not got on purpose now
Into the window to look after me.
I have no power to go now, and I should be hanged.   15
Farewell all business, I desire no more
Than I see yonder. Let the goods at quay
Look to themselves; why should I toil my youth out?
It is but begging two or three year sooner,
And stay with her continually – is't a match?   20
Oh fie, what a religion have I leaped into!
Get out again, for shame! The man loves best
When his care's most, that shows his zeal to love.
Fondness is but the idiot to affection,
That plays at hot-cockles with rich merchants' wives – 25
Good to make sport withal when the chest's full,
And the long warehouse cracks. 'Tis time of day
For us to be more wise; 'tis early with us,
And if they lose the morning of their affairs,
They commonly lose the best part of the day.   30
Those that are wealthy, and have got enough,
'Tis after sunset with 'em; they may rest,
Grow fat with ease, banquet, and toy and play,
When such as I enter the heat o'th'day,
And I'll do't cheerfully.
BIANCA   I perceive, sir,   35
Y'are not gone yet; I have good hope you'll stay now.
LEANTIO
Farewell, I must not.
BIANCA   Come, come, pray return.
Tomorrow, adding but a little care more,
Will dispatch all as well. Believe me, 'twill, sir.

12 *expenses* Like much of the economic language in the play, 'expense' carries both
   a financial and a sexual meaning.
13, 15 *and* if
20 *match* bargain
24 *Fondness . . . affection* Foolish infatuation ('fondness') is a mockery of real passion
   ('affection'); 'idiot' is personified, hence infatuation is like a fool or court jester
   to the monarch Affection.
25 *hot-cockles* a game like blindman's buff; also with insinuation of sexual fondling
27 *cracks* i.e. because it is so full
37 *return.* ed. (return O)

LEANTIO

I could well wish myself where you would have me;   40
But love that's wanton must be ruled awhile
By that that's careful, or all goes to ruin.
As fitting is a government in love,
As in a kingdom; where 'tis all mere lust
'Tis like an insurrection in the people   45
That, raised in self-will, wars against all reason.
But love that is respective for increase
Is like a good king, that keeps all in peace.
Once more, farewell.

BIANCA   But this one night, I prithee.

LEANTIO

Alas, I'm in for twenty, if I stay,   50
And then for forty more, I have such luck to flesh.
I never bought a horse but he bore double.
If I stay any longer, I shall turn
An everlasting spendthrift; as you love
To be maintained well, do not call me again,   55
For then I shall not care which end goes forward.
Again, farewell to thee.   *Exit*

BIANCA   Since it must, farewell too.

MOTHER

'Faith daughter, y'are to blame, you take the course
To make him an ill husband, troth you do,
And that disease is catching, I can tell you –   60
Ay, and soon taken by a young man's blood,
And that with little urging. Nay, fie, see now,
What cause have you to weep? Would I had no more,
That have lived threescore years; there were a cause
And 'twere well thought on. Trust me, y'are to blame,   65
His absence cannot last five days at utmost.
Why should those tears be fetched forth? Cannot love
Be ev'n as well expressed in a good look,
But it must see her face still in a fountain?

---

47 *respective for increase* concerned to make a profit. 'Increase' also has an implication
   of natural procreation, as opposed to 'mere lust' (l. 44).

48 *good king* a conventional compliment to King James

52 *bore double* i.e. was strong or large enough to carry two riders. Leantio refers to
   what he claims is his habitual good fortune in sex, but unwittingly also anticipates
   Bianca's infidelity with the Duke – she will then bear 'double' riders.

56 *which end goes forward* i.e. I won't care what happens (cf. Tilley, E 130); also a
   sexual connotation

69 *still* always
   fountain i.e. reflected in the waters of a fountain; but also reflected in 'tears' (l.
   67)

It shows like a country maid dressing her head   70
By a dish of water. Come, 'tis an old custom
To weep for love.

> *Enter two or three* BOYS, *and a* CITIZEN *or two,*
> *with an* APPRENTICE

BOYS
  Now they come, now they come!
2 BOY   The Duke!
3 BOY   The State!
CITIZEN
  How near, boy?
1 BOY   I'th'next street, sir, hard at hand.
CITIZEN
  You sirrah, get a standing for your mistress,   75
  The best in all the city.
APPRENTICE   I have't for her, sir,
  'Twas a thing I provided for her overnight,
  'Tis ready at her pleasure.
CITIZEN
  Fetch her to't then, away sir!   [*Exit* APPRENTICE]
BIANCA
  What's the meaning of this hurry,   80
  Can you tell, Mother?
MOTHER   What a memory
  Have I! I see by that years come upon me.
  Why, 'tis a yearly custom and solemnity,
  Religiously observed by th'Duke and State
  To St Mark's Temple, the fifteenth of April.   85
  See if my dull brains had not quite forgot it!
  'Twas happily questioned of thee, I had gone down
      else,
  Sat like a drone below, and never thought on't.
  I would not to be ten years younger again,
  That you had lost the sight; now you shall see   90
  Our Duke, a goodly gentleman of his years.

---

73 *State* the nobles of the city, next to the Duke in rank
75 *standing* a place to stand and see
78 *pleasure* The apprentice jokes on 'standing' (l. 75), or an erection, ready for her
  'pleasure'.
83 *solemnity* festival
85 The Feast of St Mark's was April 25 on the Gregorian calendar; Middleton may
  have converted it to the 15th, as England was then still on the Julian calendar.

BIANCA
  Is he old, then?
MOTHER   About some fifty-five.
BIANCA
  That's no great age in man, he's then at best
  For wisdom and for judgement.
MOTHER   The Lord Cardinal
  His noble brother, there's a comely gentleman,   95
  And greater in devotion than in blood.
BIANCA
  He's worthy to be marked.
MOTHER   You shall behold
  All our chief States of Florence; you came fortunately
  Against this solemn day.
BIANCA   I hope so always.

                        Music

MOTHER
  I hear 'em near us now; do you stand easily?   100
BIANCA
  Exceeding well, good Mother.
MOTHER   Take this stool.
BIANCA
  I need it not, I thank you.
MOTHER   Use your will, then.

Enter in great solemnity six KNIGHTS *bare-headed, then two*
CARDINALS, *and then the* LORD CARDINAL, *then the* DUKE; *after*
him the STATES *of* FLORENCE *by two and two, with variety of*
                    music and song

              Exit [all but MOTHER *and* BIANCA]

MOTHER
  How like you, daughter?
BIANCA   'Tis a noble State.
  Methinks my soul could dwell upon the reverence
  Of such a solemn and most worthy custom.   105
  Did not the Duke look up? Methought he saw us.
MOTHER
  That's ev'ryone's conceit that sees a duke:

  92 *fifty-five* King James I was fifty-five years old on 19 June 1621; if the following
     lines are more compliment to James, the allegory would soon have to end,
     considering the Duke's subsequent actions.
  95 *comely* handsome
  96 *blood* birth
  99 *Against* in time for
  107 *conceit* idea, opinion

    If he look steadfastly, he looks straight at them,
    When he perhaps, good careful gentleman,
    Never minds any; but the look he casts   110
    Is at his own intentions, and his object
    Only the public good.
BIANCA   Most likely so.
MOTHER
    Come, come, we'll end this argument below.

                                   Exeunt

Act II, Scene i

Enter HIPPOLITO, *and Lady* LIVIA *the widow*

LIVIA
    A strange affection, brother, when I think on't!
    I wonder how thou cam'st by't.
HIPPOLITO   Ev'n as easily
    As man comes by destruction, which oft-times
    He wears in his own bosom.
LIVIA   Is the world
    So populous in women, and creation   5
    So prodigal in beauty and so various?
    Yet does love turn thy point to thine own blood?
    'Tis somewhat too unkindly. Must thy eye
    Dwell evilly on the fairness of thy kindred,
    And seek not where it should? It is confined   10
    Now in a narrower prison than was made for't.
    It is allowed a stranger; and where bounty
    Is made the great man's honour, 'tis ill husbandry
    To spare, and servants shall have small thanks for't.
    So he Heaven's bounty seems to scorn and mock,   15
    That spares free means and spends of his own stock.
HIPPOLITO
    Never was man's misery so soon sewed up,

109 *careful* full of cares, responsibility
113 *argument* topic
  7 *thy point* the point of a compass needle; also a sexual connotation ('point' =
     phallus)
     blood relations, kin
  8 *unkindly* unnatural ('kind' = kin or family)
 12 *bounty* liberality, generosity
 14 *To spare* to be frugal
 16 *free means . . . stock* i.e. ignores the rest of womankind for his own family ('stock'
     = goods; family); 'spends' also = ejaculate
 17 *sewed* ed. (sow'd O). Some editors emend to 'summed'.

Counting how truly.
LIVIA   Nay, I love you so,
   That I shall venture much to keep a change from you
   So fearful as this grief will bring upon you.   20
   'Faith, it even kills me, when I see you faint
   Under a reprehension, and I'll leave it,
   Though I know nothing can be better for you.
   Prithee, sweet brother, let not passion waste
   The goodness of thy time, and of thy fortune.   25
   Thou keep'st the treasure of that life I love
   As dearly as mine own; and if you think
   My former words too bitter, which were ministered
   By truth and zeal, 'tis but a hazarding
   Of grace and virtue, and I can bring forth   30
   As pleasant fruits as sensuality wishes
   In all her teeming longings. This I can do.
HIPPOLITO
   Oh nothing that can make my wishes perfect!
LIVIA
   I would that love of yours were pawned to't, brother,
   And as soon lost that way as I could win.   35
   Sir, I could give as shrewd a lift to chastity
   As any she that wears a tongue in Florence.
   Sh'ad need be a good horsewoman, and sit fast,
   Whom my strong argument could not fling at last.
   Prithee take courage, man; though I should counsel   40
   Another to despair, yet I am pitiful
   To thy afflictions, and will venture hard –
   I will not name for what, 'tis not handsome;
   Find you the proof, and praise me.
HIPPOLITO   Then I fear me,
   I shall not praise you in haste.
LIVIA   This is the comfort,   45
   You are not the first, brother, has attempted
   Things more forbidden than this seems to be.

22 *reprehension* reprimand
24 *passion* suffering
26 *Thou keep'st* i.e. you must keep
32 *teeming* fertile, ever-increasing
33 *perfect* completed
34 *pawned to't* pledged to guarantee Livia's success
36 *give … lift* i.e. attack
   shrewd sharp, cunning
37 *wears a tongue* i.e. women who gossip also attack the chastity of others
43 *handsome* decent

I'll minister all cordials now to you,
Because I'll cheer you up, sir.
HIPPOLITO   I am past hope.
LIVIA
Love, thou shalt see me do a strange cure then,   50
As e'er was wrought on a disease so mortal,
And near akin to shame. When shall you see her?
HIPPOLITO
Never in comfort more.
LIVIA   Y'are so impatient too.
HIPPOLITO
Will you believe? Death, sh'as forsworn my company,
And sealed it with a blush.
LIVIA   So, I perceive   55
All lies upon my hands then; well, the more glory
When the work's finished.

Enter SERVANT

                          How now, sir, the news!
SERVANT
Madam, your niece, the virtuous Isabella,
Is 'lighted now to see you.
LIVIA   That's great fortune.
Sir, your stars bless. You simple, lead her in.   60
                                        Exit SERVANT
HIPPOLITO
What's this to me?
LIVIA   Your absence, gentle brother;
I must bestir my wits for you.
HIPPOLITO   Ay, to great purpose.
                                        Exit HIPPOLITO
LIVIA
Beshrew you, would I loved you not so well!
I'll go to bed, and leave this deed undone.
I am the fondest where I once affect,   65
The carefull'st of their healths, and of their ease,
    forsooth,
That I look still but slenderly to mine own.
I take a course to pity him so much now

48 *cordials* medicines which stimulate the heart
54 *believe? Death* ed. (believe death O). 'Death' is a contraction of the expletive 'by
    God's death'.
59 *'lighted* arrived
60 *simple* fool, blockhead. Some editions emend to 'bless you simply'.
65 *fondest* most foolish
    affect love

That I have none left for modesty and myself.
This 'tis to grow so liberal; y'have few sisters   70
That love their brother's ease 'bove their own honesties.
But if you question my affections,
That will be found my fault.

Enter ISABELLA *the niece*

                            Niece, your love's welcome.
Alas, what draws that paleness to thy cheeks?
This enforced marriage towards?
ISABELLA   It helps, good aunt,   75
Amongst some other griefs; but those I'll keep
Locked up in modest silence, for they're sorrows
Would shame the tongue more than they grieve the
    thought.
LIVIA
Indeed, the Ward is simple.
ISABELLA   Simple! That were well;
Why, one might make good shift with such a husband.   80
But he's a fool entailed, he halts downright in't.
LIVIA
And knowing this, I hope 'tis at your choice
To take or refuse, niece.
ISABELLA   You see it is not.
I loathe him more than beauty can hate death
Or age, her spiteful neighbour.
LIVIA   Let't appear, then.   85
ISABELLA
How can I, being born with that obedience
That must submit unto a father's will?
If he command, I must of force consent.
LIVIA
Alas, poor soul! Be not offended, prithee,
If I set by the name of niece awhile,   90
And bring in pity in a stranger fashion.
It lies here in this breast, would cross this match.

---

70 *liberal* over-generous; also a connotation of 'licentious'
73 s.d. This entrance is placed after 'This enforced marriage towards' in O.
75 *towards* approaching, imminent
80 *make good shift* succeed
81 *entailed* i.e. he has hereditary qualities which make him a fool
   halts downright stops completely at 'fool'
88 *of force* of necessity
90 *set by* set aside
92 *cross* thwart

ISABELLA
  How, cross it, aunt?
LIVIA   Ay, and give thee more liberty
  Than thou hast reason yet to apprehend.
ISABELLA
  Sweet aunt, in goodness keep not hid from me   95
  What may befriend my life.
LIVIA   Yes, yes, I must,
  When I return to reputation,
  And think upon the solemn vow I made
  To your dead mother, my most loving sister –
  As long as I have her memory 'twixt mine eyelids,   100
  Look for no pity now.
ISABELLA   Kind, sweet, dear aunt –
LIVIA
  No, 'twas a secret I have took special care of,
  Delivered by your mother on her deathbed –
  That's nine years now – and I'll not part from't yet,
  Though nev'r was fitter time, nor greater cause for't.   105
ISABELLA
  As you desire the praises of a virgin –
LIVIA
  Good sorrow! I would do thee any kindness,
  Not wronging secrecy or reputation.
ISABELLA
  Neither of which, as I have hope of fruitfulness,
  Shall receive wrong from me.
LIVIA   Nay, 'twould be your own
    wrong,   110
  As much as any's, should it come to that once.
ISABELLA
  I need no better means to work persuasion, then.
LIVIA
  Let it suffice, you may refuse this fool,
  Or you may take him, as you see occasion
  For your advantage; the best wits will do't.   115
  Y'have liberty enough in your own will,
  You cannot be enforced; there grows the flower,
  If you could pick it out, makes whole life sweet to you.
  That which you call your father's command's nothing;
  Then your obedience must needs be as little.   120

  93 *liberty* Cf. II.i.70n.
  99 *sister* i.e. sister-in-law
100 *'twixt mine eyelids* in my mind's eye
109 *fruitfulness* ed. (fruit- / ness O)

If you can make shift here to taste your happiness,
Or pick out aught that likes you, much good do you.
You see your cheer, I'll make you no set dinner.

ISABELLA
And trust me, I may starve for all the good
I can find yet in this. Sweet aunt, deal plainlier.   125

LIVIA
Say I should trust you now upon an oath,
And give you in a secret that would start you,
How am I sure of you, in faith and silence?

ISABELLA
Equal assurance may I find in mercy,
As you for that in me.

LIVIA   It shall suffice.   130
Then know, however custom has made good,
For reputation's sake, the names of niece
And aunt 'twixt you and I, w'are nothing less.

ISABELLA
How's that?

LIVIA   I told you I should start your blood.
You are no more allied to any of us,   135
Save what the courtesy of opinion casts
Upon your mother's memory, and your name,
Than the merest stranger is, or one begot
At Naples when the husband lies at Rome;
There's so much odds betwixt us. Since your
      knowledge   140
Wished more instruction, and I have your oath
In pledge for silence, it makes me talk the freelier.
Did never the report of that famed Spaniard,
Marquis of Coria, since your time was ripe
For understanding, fill your ear with wonder?   145

---

121 *make shift* make an effort, bestir yourself
   taste your happiness This carries a general sexual innuendo.
122 *likes* pleases
   do you may it do you
123 *cheer ... dinner* 'cheer' = meal, food; i.e. you see what there is, I won't describe
   it further
127 *start* startle
129 *mercy* i.e. God's divine mercy on the Day of Judgement
133 *w'are nothing less* i.e. we are not actually related
134 *start your blood* startle; sexually arouse
140 *There's ... us* i.e. there is so much distance in our relationship
144 *Marquis of Coria* The name is given in Middleton's source; Coria is a town in
   Spain.

ISABELLA
  Yes, what of him? I have heard his deeds of honour
  Often related when we lived in Naples.
LIVIA
  You heard the praises of your father then.
ISABELLA
  My father!
LIVIA   That was he. But all the business
  So carefully and so discreetly carried,   150
  That fame received no spot by't, not a blemish.
  Your mother was so wary to her end,
  None knew it but her conscience, and her friend,
  Till penitent confession made it mine,
  And now my pity, yours. It had been long else,   155
  And I hope care and love alike in you,
  Made good by oath, will see it take no wrong now.
  How weak his commands now, whom you call father?
  How vain all his enforcements, your obedience?
  And what a largeness in your will and liberty,   160
  To take, or to reject, or to do both?
  For fools will serve to father wise men's children.
  All this y'have time to think on. Oh my wench!
  Nothing o'erthrows our sex but indiscretion;
  We might do well else of a brittle people   165
  As any under the great canopy.
  I pray forget not but to call me aunt still;
  Take heed of that, it may be marked in time else.
  But keep your thoughts to yourself, from all the world,
  Kindred, or dearest friend, nay, I entreat you,   170
  From him that all this while you have called uncle;
  And though you love him dearly, as I know
  His deserts claim as much ev'n from a stranger,
  Yet let not him know this, I prithee do not –
  As ever thou hast hope of second pity,   175
  If thou shouldst stand in need on't, do not do't.

149 *business* affair; with a sexual connotation
151 *fame* reputation
152 *end* death
153 *friend* euphemism for 'lover'
160 *will and liberty* self-determination and freedom. Both words also have strong
     sexual overtones.
165 *brittle* fickle or frail
166 *great canopy* the sky; perhaps the theatre structure itself (cf. *Hamlet* II.ii.300–1:
     'the most excellent canopy, the air'). The 'canopy' was the underside of the roof
     covering part of the stage.
175 *second pity* i.e. more assistance from Livia

ISABELLA
  Believe my oath, I will not.
LIVIA   Why, well said.
  [*Aside*] Who shows more craft t'undo a maidenhead,
  I'll resign my part to her.

                Enter HIPPOLITO

[*To him*]   She's thine own, go.
                                    Exit [LIVIA]
HIPPOLITO
  [*Aside*] Alas, fair flattery cannot cure my sorrows!   180
ISABELLA
  [*Aside*] Have I passed so much time in ignorance,
  And never had the means to know myself
  Till this blest hour? Thanks to her virtuous pity
  That brought it now to light; would I had known it
  But one day sooner! He had then received   185
  In favours, what, poor gentleman, he took
  In bitter words: a slight and harsh reward
  For one of his deserts.
HIPPOLITO [*Aside*]   There seems to me now
  More anger and distraction in her looks.
  I'm gone, I'll not endure a second storm;   190
  The memory of the first is not past yet.
ISABELLA
  [*Aside*] Are you returned, you comforts of my life,
  In this man's presence? I will keep you fast now,
  And sooner part eternally from the world
  Than my good joys in you. [*To him*] Prithee, forgive me, 195
  I did but chide in jest; the best loves use it
  Sometimes, it sets an edge upon affection.
  When we invite our best friends to a feast
  'Tis not all sweetmeats that we set before them,
  There's somewhat sharp and salt, both to whet appetite, 200
  And make 'em taste their wine well. So, methinks,
  After a friendly, sharp and savoury chiding,
  A kiss tastes wondrous well, and full o'th'grape.

                [*She kisses him*]

  How think'st thou, does't not?
HIPPOLITO   'Tis so excellent,

179–80 s.d. *Enter* HIPPOLITO ... *Exit* ed. (*Exit.* / *Enter* HIPPOLITO O)
197–203 *set an edge* ... *o'th'grape* 'Edge' suggests sexual arousal. This passage equates
    sexual appetite with an appetite for food, in a string of double entendres, ending
    in a kiss.

I know not how to praise it, what to say to't.   205
ISABELLA
This marriage shall go forward.
HIPPOLITO   With the Ward!
Are you in earnest?
ISABELLA   'Twould be ill for us else.
HIPPOLITO
[*Aside*] For us? How means she that?
ISABELLA [*Aside*]   Troth, I begin
To be so well, methinks, within this hour,
For all this match able to kill one's heart,   210
Nothing can pull me down now. Should my father
Provide a worse fool yet – which I should think
Were a hard thing to compass – I'd have him either:
The worse the better, none can come amiss now,
If he want wit enough. So discretion love me,   215
Desert and judgement, I have content sufficient.
[*To him*] She that comes once to be a housekeeper
Must not look every day to fare well, sir,
Like a young waiting-gentlewoman in service;
For she feeds commonly as her lady does,   220
No good bit passes her, but she gets a taste on't.
But when she comes to keep house for herself,
She's glad of some choice cates then once a week,
Or twice at most, and glad if she can get 'em:
So must affection learn to fare with thankfulness.   225
Pray make your love no stranger, sir, that's all.
[*Aside*] Though you be one yourself, and know not on't,
And I have sworn you must not.   *Exit*
HIPPOLITO   This is beyond me!
Never came joys so unexpectedly
To meet desires in man. How came she thus?   230
What has she done to her, can any tell?
'Tis beyond sorcery, this, drugs, or love-powders;
Some art that has no name, sure, strange to me
Of all the wonders I e'er met withal

213 *compass* achieve
     either i.e. I'd have him just as willingly
215 *want* lack
215–16 *discretion . . . Desert and judgement* Hippolito's qualities
217–24 *housekeeper . . . get 'em* Another extended conflation of the language of food,
     commerce and sexuality: the 'house-keeper' is the married housewife, and the
     'young waiting-gentlewoman' is an unmarried girl.
223 *cates* delicacies, as opposed to simple food
231 *she* refers to Livia

Throughout my ten years' travels; but I'm thankful
   for't.   235
This marriage now must of necessity forward;
It is the only veil wit can devise
To keep our acts hid from sin-piercing eyes.   *Exit*

Act II, Scene ii

Enter GUARDIANO *and* LIVIA

LIVIA
  How, sir, a gentlewoman so young, so fair
  As you set forth, spied from the widow's window!
GUARDIANO
  She!
LIVIA Our Sunday-dinner woman?
GUARDIANO
  And Thursday-supper woman, the same still.
  I know not how she came by her, but I'll swear   5
  She's the prime gallant for a face in Florence;
  And no doubt other parts follow their leader.
  The Duke himself first spied her at the window;
  Then in a rapture, as if admiration
  Were poor when it were single, beckoned me,   10
  And pointed to the wonder warily,
  As one that feared she would draw in her splendour
  Too soon, if too much gazed at. I nev'r knew him
  So infinitely taken with a woman,
  Nor can I blame his appetite, or tax   15
  His raptures of slight folly; she's a creature
  Able to draw a State from serious business,
  And make it their best piece to do her service.
  What course shall we devise? H'as spoke twice now.

---

  2 *spied from* she looked out from; she was seen at. The ambiguous grammar suggests
    that she did the spying, *and* that she was the object spied.
  3–4 *Sunday-dinner . . . Thursday-supper* The Mother was probably entertained twice
    a week as an act of charity.
  6 *prime* top, best
    gallant male or female fashionable person
  7 *leader* i.e. her 'face'
  10 *single* unshared
  15–16 *tax . . . folly* criticize his passion as trivial folly
  18 *piece* work, accomplishment

LIVIA
  Twice?
GUARDIANO   'Tis beyond your apprehension   20
  How strangely that one look has catched his heart!
  'Twould prove but too much worth in wealth and
    favour
  To those should work his peace.
LIVIA   And if I do't not,
  Or at least come as near it – if your art
  Will take a little pains and second me –   25
  As any wench in Florence of my standing,
  I'll quite give o'er, and shut up shop in cunning.
GUARDIANO
  'Tis for the Duke, and if I fail your purpose,
  All means to come, by riches or advancement,
  Miss me and skip me over!
LIVIA   Let the old woman then   30
  Be sent for with all speed, then I'll begin.
GUARDIANO
  A good conclusion follow, and a sweet one,
  After this stale beginning with old ware.
  Within there!

Enter SERVANT

SERVANT   Sir, do you call?
GUARDIANO   Come near, list hither.

[*Talks aside with* SERVANT]

LIVIA
  I long myself to see this absolute creature,   35
  That wins the heart of love and praise so much.
GUARDIANO
  Go, sir, make haste.
LIVIA   Say I entreat her company;
  Do you hear, sir?
SERVANT   Yes, madam.   *Exit*
LIVIA   That brings her quickly.
GUARDIANO
  I would 'twere done; the Duke waits the good hour,
  And I wait the good fortune that may spring from't.   40
  I have had a lucky hand these fifteen year

20 *apprehension* ed. (apprehension. O)   21 *strangely* ed. (strangly O)
23 *work his peace* satisfy his desires
33 *stale . . . ware* old goods, i.e. the Mother   35 *absolute* complete, perfect

At such court-passage with three dice in a dish.
Signor Fabritio!

Enter FABRITIO

FABRITIO
Oh sir, I bring an alteration in my mouth now.
GUARDIANO
[*Aside*] An alteration! No wise speech, I hope;   45
He means not to talk wisely, does he trow?
[*To him*] Good! What's the change, I pray, sir?
FABRITIO   A new
    change.
GUARDIANO
[*Aside*] Another yet! 'Faith, there's enough already.
FABRITIO
My daughter loves him now.
GUARDIANO   What, does she, sir?
FABRITIO
Affects him beyond thought, who but the Ward,
    forsooth!   50
No talk but of the Ward; she would have him
To choose 'bove all the men she ever saw.
My will goes not so fast as her consent now;
Her duty gets before my command still.
GUARDIANO
Why then, sir, if you'll have me speak my thoughts,   55
I smell 'twill be a match.
FABRITIO   Ay, and a sweet young couple,
If I have any judgement.
GUARDIANO [*Aside*]   'Faith, that's little.
[*To him*] Let her be sent tomorrow before noon,
And handsomely tricked up; for 'bout that time
I mean to bring her in and tender her to him.   60
FABRITIO
I warrant you for handsome; I will see
Her things laid ready, every one in order,

---

42 *court-passage* 'Passage is a Game at Dice to be play'd at but by two, and it is
    performed with three Dice. The *Caster* throws continually till he hath thrown
    Doubles under ten, and then he is out and loseth; or doublets above ten, and
    then he *passeth* and wins' (Charles Cotton, *Compleat Gamester* [1674], p. 167;
    quoted in Gill). 'Court passage' also suggests sexual encounters at Court; 'three
    dice in a dish' also carries a sexual insinuation.
47 *new change* a comical redundancy; perhaps also a reference to the so-called New
    'Change' (an addition to the Royal Exchange), a meeting-place for merchants,
    opened in the Strand in 1609, which some thought unnecessary
59 *tricked up* dressed up

And have some part of her tricked up tonight.
GUARDIANO
Why, well said.
FABRITIO   'Twas a use her mother had,
When she was invited to an early wedding;   65
She'd dress her head o'ernight, sponge up herself,
And give her neck three lathers.
GUARDIANO [*Aside*]   Ne'er a halter?
FABRITIO
On with her chain of pearl, her ruby bracelets,
Lay ready all her tricks and jiggam-bobs.
GUARDIANO
So must your daughter.
FABRITIO   I'll about it straight, sir.   70

          Exit

LIVIA
How he sweats in the foolish zeal of fatherhood
After six ounces an hour, and seems
To toil as much as if his cares were wise ones!
GUARDIANO
Y'have let his folly blood in the right vein, lady.
LIVIA
And here comes his sweet son-in-law that shall be.   75
They're both allied in wit before the marriage;
What will they be hereafter, when they are nearer?
Yet they can go no further than the fool:
There's the world's end in both of 'em.

          Enter WARD *and* SORDIDO, *one with a shuttle-*
          cock, the other a battledore

GUARDIANO   Now, young heir!
WARD
What's the next business after shittlecock now?   80

64 *use* custom
67 *halter* A halter would be made of leather (thus the pun on 'lather'); halters are for horses, cows and people going to be hanged.
69 *tricks and jiggam-bobs* ornaments and knick-knacks. 'Tricks' also has a sexual connotation. Cf. also 'tricked' (l. 59) and 'tricks' (l. 188).
72 *After* at the rate of
74 *let ... blood* reference to blood-letting as a medical cure; used here figuratively, as Livia has precisely described Fabritio's 'foolish zeal'
79 *world's end* i.e. as far as one can go
   s.d. *shuttlecock* ed. (shittlecock O). This edition retains the Ward's mispronunciations; the excretory pun is explicitly invoked in 'stool-ball' at III.iii.87. *shuttlecock ... battledore* The 'shuttlecock' is struck back and forth by a racquet, or 'battledore', in this precursor game to modern badminton. The Ward, at ll.

GUARDIANO
Tomorrow you shall see the gentlewoman
Must be your wife.
WARD   There's ev'n another thing too
Must be kept up with a pair of battledores.
My wife! What can she do?
GUARDIANO
Nay, that's a question you should ask yourself, Ward,   85
When y'are alone together.

                [LIVIA *and* GUARDIANO *talk apart*]

WARD   That's as I list.
A wife's to be asked anywhere, I hope;
I'll ask her in a congregation, if I have a mind to't, and
so save a licence. My guardianer has no more wit than
an herb-woman that sells away all her sweet herbs and   90
nosegays, and keeps a stinking breath for her own
pottage.
SORDIDO
Let me be at the choosing of your beloved,
If you desire a woman of good parts.
WARD
Thou shalt, sweet Sordido.   95
SORDIDO
I have a plaguey guess: let me alone to see what she is. If
I but look upon her – 'way, I know all the faults to a hair
that you may refuse her for.
WARD
Dost thou? I prithee let me hear 'em, Sordido.
SORDIDO
Well, mark 'em then; I have 'em all in rhyme.   100
The wife your guardianer ought to tender
Should be pretty, straight and slender;
Her hair not short, her foot not long,
Her hand not huge, nor too too loud her tongue;

82–4, *will make the equation* women = shuttlecocks = whores, *because women
supposedly 'shuttle' back and forth between 'cocks', to 'do', and are 'kept up' by
phallic 'battledores'.*

82 *thing* i.e. phallus

87 *asked* ed. (ask O)

88–9 *ask . . . licence* He will proclaim the banns of marriage publicly, and so save the
expense of a special licence.

91–2 *breath . . . pottage* blowing on soup to cool it

96 *plaguey guess* shrewd or sharp judgement

97 *'way* straightaway, immediately

No pearl in eye, nor ruby in her nose,   105
No burn or cut, but what the catalogue shows.
She must have teeth, and that no black ones,
And kiss most sweet when she does smack once;
Her skin must be both white and plumped,
Her body straight, not hopper-rumped,   110
Or wriggle sideways like a crab;
She must be neither slut nor drab,
Nor go too splay-foot with her shoes,
To make her smock lick up the dews.
And two things more, which I forgot to tell ye: 115
She neither must have bump in back, nor belly.
These are the faults that will not make her pass.

WARD
And if I spy not these, I am a rank ass.

SORDIDO
Nay more; by right, sir, you should see her naked,
For that's the ancient order.

WARD   See her naked?   120
That were good sport, i'faith. I'll have the books turned
    over;
And if I find her naked on record,
She shall not have a rag on. But stay, stay,
How if she should desire to see me so, too?
I were in a sweet case then, such a foul skin.   125

SORDIDO
But y'have a clean shirt, and that makes amends, sir.

WARD
I will not see her naked for that trick, though.   *Exit*

SORDIDO
Then take her with all faults, with her clothes on!
And they may hide a number with a bum-roll.

---

105 *pearl in eye* whitish spot in eye, the result of a cataract or a disease like smallpox
    ruby i.e. pimple
106 *burn or cut* To 'burn' is a symptom of venereal disease; 'cut' = slang for female
    genitals (cf. Malvolio in *Twelfth Night* II.v.86–8).
109 *plumped* ed. (plump O)
110 *hopper-rumped* 'The hopper of a mill is shaped like an inverted pyramid and has
    a hopping or shaking movement' (Gill) – i.e. with large buttocks.
112 *drab* whore
116 *have bump . . . belly* be neither hunchbacked nor pregnant
119–25 *naked . . . skin* This custom is described in Thomas More's *Utopia*, but the
    passage also says the male wooer should appear naked to the woman, as the Ward
    fears.
125 *case* situation; clothing
129 *bum-roll* a cushion worn to hold out the skirt

'Faith, choosing of a wench in a huge farthingale   130
Is like the buying of ware under a great penthouse:
What with the deceit of one,
And the false light of th'other, mark my speeches,
He may have a diseased wench in's bed,
And rotten stuff in's breeches.   *Exit* 135

GUARDIANO
It may take handsomely.
LIVIA   I see small hindrance.
How now, so soon returned?

Enter MOTHER

GUARDIANO   She's come.
LIVIA   That's well.
Widow, come, come, I have a great quarrel to you,
'Faith, I must chide you, that you must be sent for!
You make yourself so strange, never come at us;   140
And yet so near a neighbour, and so unkind!
Troth, y'are to blame, you cannot be more welcome
To any house in Florence, that I'll tell you.

MOTHER
My thanks must needs acknowledge so much, madam.

LIVIA
How can you be so strange then? I sit here   145
Sometime whole days together without company,
When business draws this gentleman from home,
And should be happy in society,
Which I so well affect as that of yours.
I know y'are alone, too; why should not we,   150
Like two kind neighbours, then supply the wants
Of one another, having tongue-discourse,
Experience in the world, and such kind helps
To laugh down time, and meet age merrily?

MOTHER
Age, madam! You speak mirth; 'tis at my door,   155

---

130 *farthingale* a framework of hoops, worn about the waist, which extended a
    woman's dress
131 *penthouse* a sloping roof over a door or window. It would block the light from a
    merchant's shop, hence make it more difficult to judge the quality of his goods
    in such a 'false light' (l. 133).
135 *rotten stuff* poor quality cloth; venereal disease
136 *take* work, succeed
140 *so strange* so much a stranger
152 *tongue-discourse* facility in conversation
154 *merrily* ed. (merely O)

But a long journey from your ladyship yet.

LIVIA
My faith, I'm nine and thirty, ev'ry stroke, wench,
And 'tis a general observation
'Mongst knights' wives or widows, we accompt
Ourselves then old, when young men's eyes leave
    looking at's.   160
'Tis a true rule amongst us, and ne'er failed yet
In any but in one, that I remember;
Indeed, she had a friend at nine and forty;
Marry, she paid well for him, and in th'end
He kept a quean or two with her own money,   165
That robbed her of her plate and cut her throat.

MOTHER
She had her punishment in this world, madam,
And a fair warning to all other women
That they live chaste at fifty.

LIVIA   Ay, or never, wench.
Come, now I have thy company I'll not part with't   170
Till after supper.

MOTHER   Yes, I must crave pardon, madam.

LIVIA
I swear you shall stay supper. We have no strangers,
    woman,
None but my sojourners and I, this gentleman
And the young heir his ward; you know our company.

MOTHER
Some other time I will make bold with you, madam.   175

GUARDIANO
Nay, pray stay, widow.

LIVIA   'Faith, she shall not go;
Do you think I'll be forsworn?

Table and chess [are prepared]

MOTHER   'Tis a great while
Till supper time; I'll take my leave then, now, madam,
And come again i'th'evening, since your ladyship
Will have it so.

LIVIA   I'th'evening! By my troth, wench,   180

---

163 *friend* lover. See II.i.153n.
165 *quean* whore
166 *plate* silver dishes and cutlery
168 *fair ... women* perhaps an allusion to the anonymous play *A Warning for Fair Women* (1599)
173 *sojourners* house guests staying with her

I'll keep you while I have you; you have great business,
   sure,
To sit alone at home; I wonder strangely
What pleasure you take in't! Were't to me now,
I should be ever at one neighbour's house
Or other all day long. Having no charge,   185
Or none to chide you, if you go, or stay,
Who may live merrier, ay, or more at heart's ease?
Come, we'll to chess, or draughts; there are an hundred
   tricks
To drive out time till supper, never fear't, wench.
MOTHER
I'll but make one step home, and return straight,
   madam.   190
LIVIA
Come, I'll not trust you; you use more excuses
To your kind friends than ever I knew any.
What business can you have, if you be sure
Y'have locked the doors? And that being all you have,
I know y'are careful on't. One afternoon   195
So much to spend here! Say I should entreat you now
To lie a night or two, or a week with me,
Or leave your own house for a month together –
It were a kindness that long neighbourhood
And friendship might well hope to prevail in.   200
Would you deny such a request? I'faith,
Speak truth, and freely.
MOTHER   I were then uncivil, madam.
LIVIA
Go to then, set your men; we'll have whole nights
Of mirth together ere we be much older, wench.
MOTHER
[*Aside*] As good now tell her, then, for she will know't;   205
I have always found her a most friendly lady.
LIVIA
Why, widow, where's your mind?
MOTHER   Troth, ev'n at home,
   madam.
To tell you truth, I left a gentlewoman
Ev'n sitting all alone, which is uncomfortable,

182 *strangely* greatly
185 *charge* responsibility, duty
188 *chess* Middleton was technically knowledgeable about chess; his play *A Game At Chess* (1624), an allegory of English/Spanish foreign relations, would become the most popular play of the period.
203 *men* chessmen

Especially to young bloods.
LIVIA   Another excuse!   210
MOTHER
No, as I hope for health, madam, that's a truth;
Please you to send and see.
LIVIA   What gentlewoman? Pish!
MOTHER
Wife to my son, indeed, but not known, madam,
To any but yourself.
LIVIA   Now I beshrew you,
Could you be so unkind to her and me,   215
To come and not bring her? 'Faith, 'tis not friendly.
MOTHER
I feared to be too bold.
LIVIA   Too bold? Oh what's become
Of the true hearty love was wont to be
'Mongst neighbours in old time?
MOTHER   And she's a stranger,
      madam.
LIVIA
The more should be her welcome. When is courtesy   220
In better practice, than when 'tis employed
In entertaining strangers? I could chide, i'faith.
Leave her behind, poor gentlewoman, alone too!
Make some amends, and send for her betimes, go.
MOTHER
Please you command one of your servants, madam.   225
LIVIA
Within there.

Enter SERVANT

SERVANT   Madam.
LIVIA   Attend the gentlewoman.
MOTHER
[*Aside*] It must be carried wondrous privately
From my son's knowledge, he'll break out in storms
      else.
[*To* SERVANT] Hark you, sir.

[*They talk privately; exit* SERVANT]

LIVIA [*Aside to* GUARDIANO]   Now comes in the heat
      of your part.

---

224 *betimes* at once
229–30 *part . . . out* a theatrical metaphor: to 'be out' is to forget the lines of a 'part'

GUARDIANO
    [Aside to LIVIA] True, I know it, lady, and if I be out,   230
    May the Duke banish me from all employments,
    Wanton, or serious.
LIVIA   So, have you sent, widow?
MOTHER
    Yes, madam, he's almost at home by this.
LIVIA
    And 'faith, let me entreat you, that henceforward
    All such unkind faults may be swept from friendship,   235
    Which does but dim the lustre. And think thus much,
    It is a wrong to me, that have ability
    To bid friends welcome, when you keep 'em from me;
    You cannot set greater dishonour near me,
    For bounty is the credit and the glory   240
    Of those that have enough. I see y'are sorry,
    And the good 'mends is made by't.
MOTHER   Here she's, madam.

        Enter BIANCA, *and* SERVANT [*who*
          shows her in, then exits]

BIANCA
    [Aside] I wonder how she comes to send for me now?
LIVIA
    Gentlewoman, y'are most welcome, trust me y'are,
    As courtesy can make one, or respect   245
    Due to the presence of you.
BIANCA   I give you thanks, lady.
LIVIA
    I heard you were alone, and 't had appeared
    An ill condition in me, though I knew you not,
    Nor ever saw you – yet humanity
    Thinks ev'ry case her own – to have kept your company 250
    Here from you, and left you all solitary.
    I rather ventured upon boldness then
    As the least fault, and wished your presence here –
    A thing most happily motioned of that gentleman,
    Whom I request you, for his care and pity,   255
    To honour and reward with your acquaintance;
    A gentleman that ladies' rights stands for,

242 *'mends* amends
248 *ill condition* bad manners
249 *humanity* humaneness
254 *motioned of* proposed by
257 *stands for* professes or defends; has an erection

That's his profession.
BIANCA   'Tis a noble one,
And honours my acquaintance.
GUARDIANO   All my intentions
Are servants to such mistresses.
BIANCA   'Tis your modesty   260
It seems, that makes your deserts speak so low, sir.
LIVIA
Come, widow. [*To* BIANCA] Look you, lady, here's our
    business;
Are we not well employed, think you?

                    [*Points to chess table*]
                                        An old quarrel
Between us, that will never be at an end.
BIANCA   No,
And methinks there's men enough to part you, lady.   265
LIVIA
Ho! But they set us on, let us come off
As well as we can, poor souls, men care no farther.
I pray sit down, forsooth, if you have the patience
To look upon two weak and tedious gamesters.
GUARDIANO
'Faith, madam, set these by till evening,   270
You'll have enough on't then; the gentlewoman,
Being a stranger, would take more delight
To see your rooms and pictures.
LIVIA   Marry, good sir,
And well remembered! I beseech you show 'em her;
That will beguile time well. Pray heartily do, sir,   275
I'll do as much for you; here, take these keys,
Show her the monument too – and that's a thing
Everyone sees not; you can witness that, widow.
MOTHER
And that's worth sight indeed, madam.
BIANCA   Kind lady,
I fear I came to be a trouble to you.   280

258 *profession* an ironic reference to Guardiano's 'profession' as guardian, as well as
    his assertion. See note at I.ii.3.
258–9 *one, / And* ed. (one, and O)
259–60 *intentions / Are* ed. (intentions are O)
264–5 *No, / And* ed. (No, and O)
265 *men* chessmen
266 *set us on* encourage or incite; sexually arouse
    come off come through, get free; achieve sexual orgasm
277 *monument* a carved figure in wood or stone

LIVIA
  Oh nothing less, forsooth.
BIANCA   And to this courteous
    gentleman,
  That wears a kindness in his breast so noble
  And bounteous to the welcome of a stranger.
GUARDIANO
  If you but give acceptance to my service,
  You do the greatest grace and honour to me   285
  That courtesy can merit.
BIANCA   I were to blame else,
  And out of fashion much. I pray you lead, sir.
LIVIA
  After a game or two w'are for you, gentlefolks.
GUARDIANO
  We wish no better seconds in society
  Than your discourses, madam, and your partner's
    there.   290
MOTHER
  I thank your praise. I listened to you, sir,
  Though when you spoke there came a paltry rook
  Full in my way, and chokes up all my game.
                    Exit GUARDIANO *and* BIANCA
LIVIA
  Alas, poor widow, I shall be too hard for thee.
MOTHER
  Y'are cunning at the game, I'll be sworn, madam.   295
LIVIA
  It will be found so, ere I give you over.
  She that can place her man well –
MOTHER   As you do, madam.
LIVIA
  – As I shall, wench, can never lose her game.
  Nay, nay, the black king's mine.
MOTHER   Cry you mercy, madam.

281 *nothing less* i.e. not at all
292 *rook* the chesspiece, now also known as the castle. In Middleton's time, it was
     also called the 'duke' (see l. 300).
295 *game* the chessgame, but here – as throughout this scene – with an obvious sexual
     connotation as well
296 *ere . . . over* before I am finished with you
297 *man* the chesspiece; the duke offstage
299 *black king* the chesspiece, here associated with evil, in contrast to the 'saintish'
     'white king' at l. 305
     Cry you mercy The rules of modern chess require a similar phrase if a player
     accidentally touches the wrong piece.

LIVIA
    And this my queen.
MOTHER   I see't now.
LIVIA   Here's a duke   300
    Will strike a sure stroke for the game anon;
    Your pawn cannot come back to relieve itself.
MOTHER
    I know that, madam.
LIVIA   You play well the whilst;
    How she belies her skill! I hold two ducats
    I give you check and mate to your white king,   305
    Simplicity itself, your saintish king there.
MOTHER
    Well, ere now, lady,
    I have seen the fall of subtlety. Jest on.
LIVIA
    Ay, but simplicity receives two for one.
MOTHER
    What remedy but patience!

                Enter above GUARDIANO *and* BIANCA

BIANCA   Trust me, sir,   310
    Mine eye nev'r met with fairer ornaments.
GUARDIANO
    Nay, livelier, I'm persuaded, neither Florence
    Nor Venice can produce.
BIANCA   Sir, my opinion
    Takes your part highly.
GUARDIANO   There's a better piece
    Yet than all these.

                [*Enter*] DUKE *above*

BIANCA   Not possible, sir!
GUARDIANO   Believe it;   315
    You'll say so when you see't. Turn but your eye now,
    Y'are upon't presently.   *Exit*
BIANCA [*Sees* DUKE]   Oh sir!
DUKE   He's gone, beauty!

301 *stroke* blow; also a sexual connotation
302 *pawn . . . back* A pawn can move only forward; thus Bianca cannot escape or go
    back.
304 *hold* wager
309 *simplicity . . . one* Livia, playing black, seems to have taken 'two' of the white
    ('simplicity') pieces for 'one' of her black ones.
314 *Takes your part* supports your argument
317 *presently* immediately

Pish, look not after him! He's but a vapour
That when the sun appears is seen no more.
BIANCA
Oh treachery to honour!
DUKE   Prithee, tremble not;   320
I feel thy breast shake like a turtle panting
Under a loving hand that makes much on't.
Why art so fearful? As I'm friend to brightness,
There's nothing but respect and honour near thee.
You know me, you have seen me; here's a heart   325
Can witness I have seen thee.
BIANCA   The more's my danger.
DUKE
The more's thy happiness. Pish, strive not, sweet!
This strength were excellent employed in love, now,
But here 'tis spent amiss. Strive not to seek
Thy liberty and keep me still in prison.   330
I'faith, you shall not out till I'm released now;
We'll be both freed together, or stay still by't;
So is captivity pleasant.
BIANCA   Oh my lord!
DUKE
I am not here in vain; have but the leisure
To think on that, and thou'lt be soon resolved.   335
The lifting of thy voice is but like one
That does exalt his enemy, who, proving high,
Lays all the plots to confound him that raised him.
Take warning, I beseech thee; thou seem'st to me
A creature so composed of gentleness   340
And delicate meekness, such as bless the faces
Of figures that are drawn for goddesses,
And makes art proud to look upon her work;
I should be sorry the least force should lay
An unkind touch upon thee.
BIANCA   Oh my extremity!   345
My lord, what seek you?
DUKE   Love.
BIANCA   'Tis gone already,
I have a husband.
DUKE   That's a single comfort;

321 *turtle* turtle-dove
323 *brightness* beauty
327 *happiness* personal well-being; good fortune
337 *exalt* raise; sexually arouse (continued in 'raised', l. 338)

Take a friend to him.
BIANCA   That's a double mischief,
 Or else there's no religion.
DUKE   Do not tremble
 At fears of thine own making.
BIANCA   Nor, great lord,   350
 Make me not bold with death and deeds of ruin
 Because they fear not you; me they must fright,
 Then am I best in health. Should thunder speak
 And none regard it, it had lost the name
 And were as good be still. I'm not like those   355
 That take their soundest sleeps in greatest tempests;
 Then wake I most, the weather fearfullest,
 And call for strength to virtue.
DUKE   Sure I think
 Thou know'st the way to please me. I affect
 A passionate pleading 'bove an easy yielding,   360
 But never pitied any; they deserve none
 That will not pity me. I can command:
 Think upon that. Yet if thou truly knewest
 The infinite pleasure my affection takes
 In gentle, fair entreatings, when love's businesses   365
 Are carried courteously 'twixt heart and heart,
 You'd make more haste to please me.
BIANCA   Why should you
   seek, sir,
 To take away that you can never give?
DUKE
 But I give better in exchange: wealth, honour.
 She that is fortunate in a duke's favour   370
 Lights on a tree that bears all women's wishes;
 If your own mother saw you pluck fruit there,
 She would commend your wit and praise the time
 Of your nativity. Take hold of glory.
 Do not I know y'have cast away your life   375
 Upon necessities, means merely doubtful

---

348 *friend* lover. See II.i.153n.
    to in addition to
351 *bold with* be presumptuous of; take liberties with
353–8 She is in best (moral) health when she pays attention to, or feels 'fright' at, the
    'thunder' (l. 353) and 'greatest tempests' (l. 356) of moral prohibition. She will
    'wake' (l. 357) most when the greatest ('fearfullest') temptations – as now – are
    present.
371–2 *tree ... fruit* an allusion to the Fall, described in Genesis 3, when Eve ate of
    the fruit of the tree against God's command
376 *merely* completely

To keep you in indifferent health and fashion –
A thing I heard too lately, and soon pitied –
And can you be so much your beauty's enemy
To kiss away a month or two in wedlock,   380
And weep whole years in wants for ever after?
Come, play the wise wench, and provide for ever;
Let storms come when they list, they find thee sheltered.
Should any doubt arise, let nothing trouble thee;
Put trust in our love for the managing   385
Of all to thy heart's peace. We'll talk together,
And show a thankful joy for both our fortunes.

                                        Exit [both] above

LIVIA
Did not I say my duke would fetch you over, widow?
MOTHER
I think you spoke in earnest when you said it, madam.
LIVIA
And my black king makes all the haste he can, too.   390
MOTHER
Well, madam, we may meet with him in time yet.
LIVIA
I have given thee blind mate twice.
MOTHER   You may see,
    madam,
My eyes begin to fail.
LIVIA   I'll swear they do, wench.

                    Enter GUARDIANO

GUARDIANO
[*Aside*] I can but smile as often as I think on't,
How prettily the poor fool was beguiled,   395
How unexpectedly! It's a witty age.
Never were finer snares for women's honesties
Than are devised in these days; no spider's web
Made of a daintier thread than are now practised
To catch love's flesh-fly by the silver wing.   400
Yet to prepare her stomach by degrees
To Cupid's feast, because I saw 'twas queasy,
I showed her naked pictures by the way –

382 *wise* ed. (wife O)
388 *fetch you over* i.e. get the better of you
392 *blind mate* when your opponent places you in checkmate but does not see it,
    calling out only 'check' (Livia is the one who has blinded her opponent, of
    course); also a reference to the sexual mating offstage
400 *flesh-fly* the blow-fly, which deposits its eggs in flesh; also a sexual connotation
401 *stomach* sexual appetite

A bit to stay the appetite. Well, advancement!
I venture hard to find thee; if thou com'st   405
With a greater title set upon thy crest,
I'll take that first cross patiently, and wait
Until some other comes greater than that.
I'll endure all.

LIVIA
The game's ev'n at the best now; you may see, widow,   410
How all things draw to an end.

MOTHER   Ev'n so do I, madam.

LIVIA
I pray take some of your neighbours along with you.

MOTHER
They must be those are almost twice your years, then,
If they be chose fit matches for my time, madam.

LIVIA
Has not my duke bestirred himself?

MOTHER   Yes, 'faith, madam;   415
H'as done me all the mischief in this game.

LIVIA
H'as showed himself in's kind.

MOTHER   In's kind, call you it?
I may swear that.

LIVIA   Yes 'faith, and keep your oath.

GUARDIANO
[Aside] Hark, list! There's somebody coming down; 'tis
she.

Enter BIANCA

BIANCA
[Aside] Now bless me from a blasting! I saw that now   420
Fearful for any woman's eye to look on.
Infectious mists and mildews hang at's eyes,
The weather of a doomsday dwells upon him.

404 *stay* settle; enhance
406–8 *greater ... that* i.e. if reward comes to one more elevated (with 'greater title'),
    he will endure such a disappointment ('cross') in the hope of an even 'greater'
    reward later
411 *to an end* the end of the chessgame; the sexual climax off-stage. The Mother also
    understands Livia to refer to the end of life.
414 *time* age
415–16 *madam; / H'as* ed. (Madam; h'as O)
417 *in's kind* in his own nature
420 *blasting* infection; withering under a pernicious influence
422 *Infectious ... mildews* Mists and fog were thought to cause disease.

Yet since mine honour's leprous, why should I
Preserve that fair that caused the leprosy?   425
Come, poison all at once! [*Aside to* GUARDIANO] Thou in
    whose baseness
The bane of virtue broods, I'm bound in soul
Eternally to curse thy smooth-browed treachery,
That wore the fair veil of a friendly welcome,
And I a stranger; think upon't, 'tis worth it.   430
Murders piled up upon a guilty spirit
At his last breath will not lie heavier
Than this betraying act upon thy conscience.
Beware of off'ring the first-fruits to sin:
His weight is deadly who commits with strumpets   435
After they have been abased and made for use;
If they offend to th'death, as wise men know,
How much more they, then, that first make 'em so?
I give thee that to feed on. I'm made bold now,
I thank thy treachery; sin and I'm acquainted,   440
No couple greater; and I'm like that great one
Who, making politic use of a base villain,
He likes the treason well, but hates the traitor;
So I hate thee, slave.
GUARDIANO [*Aside*]   Well, so the Duke loves me,
I fare not much amiss then; two great feasts   445
Do seldom come together in one day,
We must not look for 'em.
BIANCA   What, at it still, Mother?
MOTHER
You see we sit by't; are you so soon returned?
LIVIA
[*Aside*] So lively and so cheerful? A good sign, that.
MOTHER
You have not seen all since, sure?
BIANCA   That have I, Mother,   450
The monument and all. I'm so beholding
To this kind, honest, courteous gentleman,
You'd little think it, Mother, showed me all,

424 *why* ed. (who O)
425 *that fair* her beauty
427 *broods* hatches
428 *smooth-browed* i.e. hypocritical
435 *His weight is deadly* i.e. his soul is mortally guilty
    commits fornicates
437 *they* those who 'commit'
438 *'em* them (the strumpets)
443 Italics indicate a proverbial saying; see Tilley, K 64.

Had me from place to place, so fashionably;
The kindness of some people, how 't exceeds!   455
'Faith, I have seen that I little thought to see
I'th'morning when I rose.
MOTHER   Nay, so I told you
Before you saw't, it would prove worth your sight.
I give you great thanks for my daughter, sir,
And all your kindness towards her.
GUARDIANO   Oh good widow!   460
Much good may 't do her – [*Aside*] forty weeks hence,
i'faith.

Enter SERVANT

LIVIA
Now, sir?
SERVANT   May't please you, madam, to walk in?
Supper's upon the table.
LIVIA   Yes, we come;
Will't please you, gentlewoman?
BIANCA   Thanks, virtuous lady –
[*Aside to* LIVIA] Y'are a damned bawd! [*Aloud to
others*] I'll follow you forsooth,   465
Pray take my mother in. [*Aside*] An old ass go with you!
[*Aloud*] This gentleman and I vow not to part.
LIVIA
Then get you both before.
BIANCA [*Aside*]   There lies his art.
              Exeunt [BIANCA, GUARDIANO, *and* SERVANT]
LIVIA
Widow, I'll follow you.   [*Exit* MOTHER]
              Is't so, 'damned bawd'?
Are you so bitter? 'Tis but want of use;   470
Her tender modesty is sea-sick a little,
Being not accustomed to the breaking billow
Of woman's wavering faith, blown with temptations.
'Tis but a qualm of honour, 'twill away;
A little bitter for the time, but lasts not.   475
Sin tastes at the first draught like wormwood water,
But drunk again, 'tis nectar ever after.   *Exit*

454 *Had me* brought me; had me sexually
461 *may 't* ed. (may O)
468 *There lies his art* As a pander, Guardiano goes 'before' the Duke.
471–2 *sea-sick . . . breaking billow* The implied voyage is a metaphor of the first sexual
    encounter.
476 *wormwood water* a drink prepared from the herb wormwood, known for its
    bitterness

Act III, Scene i

Enter MOTHER

MOTHER

I would my son would either keep at home,
Or I were in my grave!
She was but one day abroad, but ever since
She's grown so cutted, there's no speaking to her.
Whether the sight of great cheer at my lady's   5
And such mean fare at home work discontent in her,
I know not, but I'm sure she's strangely altered.
I'll nev'r keep daughter-in-law i'th'house with me
Again, if I had an hundred. When read I of any
That agreed long together, but she and her mother   10
Fell out in the first quarter? Nay, sometime
A grudging of a scolding the first week, by'r Lady.
So takes the new disease methinks in my house.
I'm weary of my part, there's nothing likes her;
I know not how to please her here a-late.   15
And here she comes.

Enter BIANCA

BIANCA   This is the strangest house
For all defects, as ever gentlewoman
Made shift withal to pass away her love in.
Why is there not a cushion-cloth of drawn work,
Or some fair cut-work pinned up in my bedchamber,   20
A silver-and-gilt casting-bottle hung by't?
Nay, since I am content to be so kind to you
To spare you for a silver basin and ewer,
Which one of my fashion looks for of duty –
She's never offered under, where she sleeps –   25

2–3 *grave! / She* ed. (grave; she O)
4 *cutted* curt, snappish
12 *grudging* a small portion
13 *new disease* a fashionable phrase for any undiagnosed disease marked by fever
14 *likes* pleases
19 *drawn work* ornamental work made by drawing out some of the threads of warp
   and woof to form patterns
20 *cut-work* embroidery or lace, the pattern being 'cut' out rather than woven in
21 *casting-bottle* bottle for sprinkling perfume
23 *To spare you for* not to demand of you
   ewer a water pitcher
25 *under* less

MOTHER
  [*Aside*] She talks of things here my whole state's not
    worth.
BIANCA
  Never a green silk quilt is there i'th'house, Mother,
  To cast upon my bed?
MOTHER   No, by troth, is there,
  Nor orange tawny neither.
BIANCA   Here's a house
  For a young gentlewoman to be got with child in!   30
MOTHER
  Yes, simple though you make it, there has been three
  Got in a year in't – since you move me to't –
  And all as sweet-faced children and as lovely
  As you'll be mother of; I will not spare you.
  What, cannot children be begot, think you,   35
  Without gilt casting-bottles? Yes, and as sweet ones.
  The miller's daughter brings forth as white boys
  As she that bathes her self with milk and bean-flour.
  'Tis an old saying, 'one may keep good cheer
  In a mean house'; so may true love affect   40
  After the rate of princes, in a cottage.
BIANCA
  Troth, you speak wondrous well for your old house here;
  'Twill shortly fall down at your feet to thank you,
  Or stoop when you go to bed, like a good child,
  To ask you blessing. Must I live in want,   45
  Because my fortune matched me with your son?
  Wives do not give away themselves to husbands,
  To the end to be quite cast away; they look
  To be the better used, and tendered rather,
  Highlier respected, and maintained the richer;   50
  They're well rewarded else for the free gift
  Of their whole life to a husband. I ask less now
  Than what I had at home when I was a maid
  And at my father's house, kept short of that

26 *state* estate
29 *orange tawny* considered a courtier's colour
37 *white boys* a term of endearment: 'darlings'
38 *bathes ... bean-flour* a sign of extreme extravagance. Cf. Middleton's *The
  Revenger's Tragedy* (III.v.84–5): the proud woman 'grieve[s] her maker / In
  sinful baths of milk, when many an infant starves'.
39 *good* ed. (gook O)
40 *affect* have its effect
48 *To the end* with the intention
49 *tendered* cherished

Which a wife knows she must have – nay, and will,   55
Will, Mother, if she be not a fool born;
And report went of me that I could wrangle
For what I wanted when I was two hours old,
And by that copy, this land still I hold.
You hear me, Mother.   *Exit*
MOTHER   Ay, too plain methinks;   60
And were I somewhat deafer when you spake
'Twere nev'r a whit the worse for my quietness.
'Tis the most suddenest, strangest alteration,
And the most subtlest that ev'r wit at threescore
Was puzzled to find out. I know no cause for't; but   65
She's no more like the gentlewoman at first
Than I am like her that nev'r lay with man yet,
And she's a very young thing where'er she be.
When she first lighted here, I told her then
How mean she should find all things; she was
     pleased, forsooth,   70
None better. I laid open all defects to her,
She was contented still. But the devil's in her,
Nothing contents her now. Tonight my son
Promised to be at home; would he were come once,
For I'm weary of my charge, and life too.   75
She'd be served all in silver, by her good will,
By night and day; she hates the name of pewterer,
More than sick men the noise, or diseased bones
That quake at fall o'th'hammer, seeming to have
A fellow-feeling with't at every blow.   80
What course shall I think on? She frets me so.

[*She withdraws to back of the stage*]

Enter LEANTIO

LEANTIO
How near am I now to a happiness
That earth exceeds not! Not another like it!
The treasures of the deep are not so precious

---

59 *copy* copyhold (the right of ownership established by custom, i.e. by her childhood
    behaviour)
69 *lighted* arrived. See II.i.59n.
74 *once* at once
77 *pewterer* Pewter is a metal of inferior quality; the making of pewter objects –
    plates, tankards – involves hammering.
78 *noise* The very 'sick' and 'diseased' are extremely sensitive to noise; there is
    possibly also a reference to 'sounds supposed to have been heard before the death
    of any person' (*English Dialect Dictionary*).

As are the concealed comforts of a man,   85
Locked up in woman's love. I scent the air
Of blessings when I come but near the house.
What a delicious breath marriage sends forth!
The violet-bed's not sweeter. Honest wedlock
Is like a banqueting-house built in a garden,   90
On which the spring's chaste flowers take delight
To cast their modest odours; when base lust
With all her powders, paintings, and best pride,
Is but a fair house built by a ditch side.
When I behold a glorious dangerous strumpet,   95
Sparkling in beauty and destruction too,
Both at a twinkling, I do liken straight
Her beautified body to a goodly temple
That's built on vaults where carcasses lie rotting;
And so by little and little I shrink back again,   100
And quench desire with a cool meditation;
And I'm as well methinks. Now for a welcome
Able to draw men's envies upon man:
A kiss now that will hang upon my lip,
As sweet as morning dew upon a rose,   105
And full as long. After a five days' fast
She'll be so greedy now, and cling about me,
I take care how I shall be rid of her;
And here't begins.

[*Enter* BIANCA; MOTHER *comes forward*]

BIANCA   Oh sir, y'are welcome home.
MOTHER
Oh is he come? I am glad on't.
LEANTIO   Is that all?   110
[*Aside*] Why this? As dreadful now as sudden death
To some rich man, that flatters all his sins
With promise of repentance when he's old,

86-9 *I scent . . . sweeter* perhaps an echo of Duncan's ironic description of Macbeth's
    castle: 'This castle hath a pleasant seat. The air / Nimbly and sweetly recommends
    itself / Unto our gentle senses' (*Macbeth* I.vi.1–3)
90 *banqueting-house* a favourite feature of Jacobean gardens; known as sites of secret
    sexual encounters
93 *pride* finery
94 *ditch side* Moorditch and the City Ditch were essentially open sewers at this time.
98-9 *goodly . . . rotting* allusion to Matthew 23:27: 'Woe unto you, scribes and
    Pharisees, hypocrites! for ye are like unto whited sepulchres, which indeed appear
    beautiful outward, but are within full of dead men's bones, and of all uncleanness'.
100 *shrink back* lose the thought; lose an erection
111 *this?* i.e. her lack of affection

And dies in the midway before he comes to't.
[*To her*] Sure y'are not well, Bianca! How dost, prithee?   115
BIANCA
I have been better than I am at this time.
LEANTIO
Alas, I thought so.
BIANCA   Nay, I have been worse too
Than now you see me, sir.
LEANTIO   I'm glad thou mend'st yet,
I feel my heart mend too. How came it to thee?
Has any thing disliked thee in my absence?   120
BIANCA
No, certain, I have had the best content
That Florence can afford.
LEANTIO   Thou makest the best on't.
Speak, Mother, what's the cause? You must needs
    know.
MOTHER
Troth, I know none, son, let her speak herself;
[*Aside*] Unless it be the same gave Lucifer   125
A tumbling cast: that's pride.
BIANCA
Methinks this house stands nothing to my mind;
I'd have some pleasant lodging i'th'high street, sir,
Or if 'twere near the court, sir, that were much better;
'Tis a sweet recreation for a gentlewoman,   130
To stand in a bay-window and see gallants.
LEANTIO
Now I have another temper, a mere stranger
To that of yours, it seems; I should delight
To see none but yourself.
BIANCA   I praise not that:
Too fond is as unseemly as too churlish;   135
I would not have a husband of that proneness
To kiss me before company, for a world.
Beside, 'tis tedious to see one thing still, sir,

120 *disliked* displeased
121–2 *best . . . afford* the greatest pleasure the city of Florence has to offer; the greatest
    sexual pleasure the Duke of Florence has to offer
125–6 *Lucifer | A* ed. (Lucifer a O)
126 *tumbling cast* wrestling throw
127 *stands nothing to my mind* is not situated as I would prefer
131 *stand in a bay-window* typical of whores, offering themselves to view in windows
132 *temper* disposition
135 *fond* foolishly infatuated
136 *proneness* tendency, inclination; also with sexual connotation (cf. I.ii.118)

Be it the best that ever heart affected;
Nay, were't yourself, whose love had power, you know,   140
To bring me from my friends, I would not stand thus
And gaze upon you always. Troth, I could not, sir;
As good be blind and have no use of sight
As look on one thing still. What's the eye's treasure,
But change of objects? You are learned, sir,   145
And know I speak not ill; 'tis full as virtuous
For woman's eye to look on several men,
As for her heart, sir, to be fixed on one.

LEANTIO
Now thou com'st home to me; a kiss for that word.

BIANCA
No matter for a kiss, sir, let it pass;   150
'Tis but a toy, we'll not so much as mind it;
Let's talk of other business and forget it.
What news now of the pirates, any stirring?
Prithee discourse a little.

MOTHER [*Aside*]   I am glad he's here yet
To see her tricks himself; I had lied monstrously   155
If I had told 'em first.

LEANTIO   Speak, what's the humour, sweet,
You make your lip so strange? This was not wont.

BIANCA
Is there no kindness betwixt man and wife
Unless they make a pigeon-house of friendship,
And be still billing? 'Tis the idlest fondness   160
That ever was invented, and 'tis pity
It's grown a fashion for poor gentlewomen;
There's many a disease kissed in a year by't,
And a French curtsy made to't. Alas, sir,
Think of the world, how we shall live; grow serious –   165
We have been married a whole fortnight now.

LEANTIO
How? A whole fortnight! Why, is that so long?

144–5 *What's . . . objects* proverbial wisdom
146 *'tis* ed. ('till O)
150 *matter* occasion
151 *toy* trifle
153 *pirates* The reference to pirates is in one of Middleton's sources, but it is also
   highly topical, as an English fleet sailed on 12 October 1620 to disperse pirates
   who were attacking English shipping routes.
157 *wont* customary
160 *fondness* foolishness
164 *French curtsy* i.e. an excessive courtesy; but also a reference to the so-called
   'French disease', syphilis (cf. l. 163)

BIANCA
'Tis time to leave off dalliance; 'tis a doctrine
Of your own teaching, if you be remembered,
And I was bound to obey it.
MOTHER [*Aside*]   Here's one fits him;   170
This was well catched, i'faith, son, like a fellow
That rids another country of a plague
And brings it home with him to his own house.

Knock within

Who knocks?
LEANTIO   Who's there now? Withdraw you, Bianca,   175
Thou art a gem no stranger's eye must see,
Howev'r thou please now to look dull on me.

Exit [BIANCA]

Enter MESSENGER

Y'are welcome, sir; to whom your business, pray?
MESSENGER
To one I see not here now.
LEANTIO   Who should that be, sir?
MESSENGER
A young gentlewoman I was sent to.
LEANTIO   A young gentle-
     woman?
MESSENGER
Ay, sir, about sixteen. Why look you wildly, sir?   180
LEANTIO
At your strange error. Y'have mistook the house, sir.
There's none such here, I assure you.
MESSENGER   I assure you too,
The man that sent me, cannot be mistook.
LEANTIO
Why, who is't sent you, sir?
MESSENGER   The Duke.
LEANTIO   The Duke?
MESSENGER
Yes, he entreats her company at a banquet   185
At Lady Livia's house.
LEANTIO   Troth, shall I tell you, sir,
It is the most erroneous business
That e'er your honest pains was abused with.
I pray forgive me, if I smile a little;
I cannot choose, i'faith, sir, at an error   190

170 *fits him* punishes him in kind
176 *please* ed. (pleas'd O)

So comical as this – I mean no harm though.
His grace has been most wondrous ill informed;
Pray so return it, sir. What should her name be?
MESSENGER
That I shall tell you straight too: Bianca Capella.
LEANTIO
How, sir, Bianca? What do you call th'other?   195
MESSENGER
Capella. Sir, it seems you know no such, then?
LEANTIO
Who should this be? I never heard o'th'name.
MESSENGER
Then 'tis a sure mistake.
LEANTIO   What if you enquired
In the next street, sir? I saw gallants there
In the new houses that are built of late.   200
Ten to one, there you find her.
MESSENGER   Nay, no matter,
I will return the mistake, and seek no further.
LEANTIO
Use your own will and pleasure, sir, y'are welcome.
                                   Exit MESSENGER
What shall I think of first? Come forth, Bianca.
Thou art betrayed, I fear me.

                    Enter BIANCA

BIANCA   Betrayed? How, sir?   205
LEANTIO
The Duke knows thee.
BIANCA   Knows me! How know you that,
    sir?
LEANTIO
H'as got thy name.
BIANCA [*Aside*]   Ay, and my good name too,
    That's worse o'th'twain.
LEANTIO   How comes this work about?
BIANCA
How should the Duke know me? Can you guess,
    Mother?
MOTHER
Not I with all my wits; sure, we kept house close.   210
LEANTIO
Kept close! Not all the locks in Italy

193 *return it* take the message back
206 *Knows me* is acquainted with me; has carnal knowledge of me

Can keep you women so. You have been gadding,
And ventured out at twilight to th'court-green yonder,
And met the gallant bowlers coming home;
Without your masks too, both of you, I'll be hanged
   else!   215
Thou hast been seen, Bianca, by some stranger;
Never excuse it.
BIANCA   I'll not seek the way, sir.
Do you think y'have married me to mew me up
Not to be seen? What would you make of me?
LEANTIO
A good wife, nothing else.
BIANCA   Why, so are some   220
That are seen ev'ry day, else the devil take 'em.
LEANTIO
No more then, I believe all virtuous in thee,
Without an argument; 'twas but thy hard chance
To be seen somewhere, there lies all the mischief.
But I have devised a riddance.
MOTHER   Now I can tell you, son,   225
The time and place.
LEANTIO   When, where?
MOTHER   What wits have I?
When you last took your leave, if you remember,
You left us both at window.
LEANTIO   Right, I know that.
MOTHER
And not the third part of an hour after,
The Duke passed by in a great solemnity   230
To St Mark's Temple, and to my apprehension
He looked up twice to th'window.
LEANTIO   Oh there quickened
The mischief of this hour!
BIANCA [Aside]   If you call't mischief,
It is a thing I fear I am conceived with.

---

212 *gadding* term frequently used to describe idle, roving women
213–14 *court-green ... bowlers* Lawn-bowling, a popular game among the nobility,
    was played on a bowling-green; here, perhaps, one near to a 'court'.
215 *masks* Italian women were expected to wear masks or veils out of doors; some
    aristocratic women in England occasionally wore masks, especially to balls and
    dances.
218 *mew* imprison, lock up
231 *apprehension* knowledge
232 *quickened* began; became pregnant. The double meaning leads to Bianca's 'con-
    ceived' (l. 234).

LEANTIO
   Looked he up twice, and could you take no warning!   235
MOTHER
   Why, once may do as much harm, son, as a thousand;
   Do not you know one spark has fired an house
   As well as a whole furnace?
LEANTIO   My heart flames for't!
   Yet let's be wise, and keep all smothered closely;
   I have bethought a means. Is the door fast?   240
MOTHER
   I locked it myself after him.
LEANTIO   You know, Mother,
   At the end of the dark parlour there's a place
   So artificially contrived for a conveyance,
   No search could ever find it. When my father
   Kept in for manslaughter, it was his sanctuary;   245
   There will I lock my life's best treasure up.
   Bianca!
BIANCA   Would you keep me closer yet?
   Have you the conscience? Y'are best ev'n choke me up,
      sir!
   You make me fearful of your health and wits,
   You cleave to such wild courses. What's the matter?   250
LEANTIO
   Why, are you so insensible of your danger
   To ask that now? The Duke himself has sent for you
   To Lady Livia's, to a banquet forsooth.
BIANCA
   Now I beshrew you heartily, has he so!
   And you the man would never yet vouchsafe   255
   To tell me on't till now. You show your loyalty
   And honesty at once; and so farewell, sir.
LEANTIO
   Bianca, whither now?
BIANCA   Why, to the Duke, sir.
   You say he sent for me.
LEANTIO   But thou dost not mean
   To go, I hope!
BIANCA   No? I shall prove unmannerly,   260
   Rude and uncivil, mad, and imitate you.
   Come, Mother, come, follow his humour no longer.

243 *artificially* artfully
        conveyance secret passage
245 *Kept ... manslaughter* stayed indoors after he had committed manslaughter
254 *beshrew* curse

We shall be all executed for treason shortly.
MOTHER
  Not I, i'faith; I'll first obey the Duke,
  And taste of a good banquet, I'm of thy mind.   265
  I'll step but up, and fetch two handkerchiefs
  To pocket up some sweetmeats, and o'ertake thee. *Exit*
BIANCA
  [*Aside*] Why, here's an old wench would trot into a bawd
    now,
  For some dry sucket or a colt in marchpane.   *Exit*
LEANTIO
  Oh thou the ripe time of man's misery, wedlock,   270
  When all his thoughts, like over-laden trees,
  Crack with the fruits they bear, in cares, in jealousies!
  Oh that's a fruit that ripens hastily,
  After 'tis knit to marriage; it begins
  As soon as the sun shines upon the bride   275
  A little to show colour. Blessed powers!
  Whence comes this alteration? The distractions,
  The fears and doubts it brings are numberless,
  And yet the cause I know not. What a peace
  Has he that never marries! If he knew   280
  The benefit he enjoyed, or had the fortune
  To come and speak with me, he should know then
  The infinite wealth he had, and discern rightly
  The greatness of his treasure by my loss.
  Nay, what a quietness has he 'bove mine,   285
  That wears his youth out in a strumpet's arms,
  And never spends more care upon a woman
  Than at the time of lust; but walks away,
  And if he find her dead at his return,
  His pity is soon done: he breaks a sigh   290
  In many parts, and gives her but a piece on't!
  But all the fears, shames, jealousies, costs and troubles,
  And still renewed cares of a marriage bed
  Live in the issue, when the wife is dead.

Enter MESSENGER

266 *handkerchiefs* used for carrying small objects
268 *trot into* turn into
269 *sucket* crystallized fruit
    colt in marchpane the figure of a young horse made out of marchpane (marzipan)
287 *spends* expends; slang term for ejaculation
294 *issue* children

MESSENGER
  A good perfection to your thoughts.
LEANTIO   The news, sir?   295
MESSENGER
  Though you were pleased of late to pin an error on me,
  You must not shift another in your stead too:
  The Duke has sent me for you.
LEANTIO   How, for me, sir?
  [*Aside*] I see then 'tis my theft; w'are both betrayed.
  Well, I'm not the first has stolen away a maid: 300
  My countrymen have used it. [*To him*] I'll along with
    you, sir.   *Exeunt*

Act III, Scene ii

A Banquet prepared. Enter GUARDIANO *and* WARD

GUARDIANO
  Take you especial note of such a gentlewoman,
  She's here on purpose; I have invited her,
  Her father, and her uncle to this banquet.
  Mark her behaviour well, it does concern you;
  And what her good parts are, as far as time   5
  And place can modestly require a knowledge of,
  Shall be laid open to your understanding.
  You know I'm both your guardian and your uncle;
  My care of you is double, ward and nephew,
  And I'll express it here.
WARD   'Faith, I should know her   10
  Now, by her mark, among a thousand women:
  A little, pretty, deft and tidy thing, you say?
GUARDIANO
  Right.
WARD   With a lusty sprouting sprig in her hair?
GUARDIANO
  Thou goest the right way still; take one mark more:
  Thou shalt nev'r find her hand out of her uncle's,   15

---

295 *good perfection* a successful conclusion
297 *shift another in your stead* try another cunning trick in your own case
301 *used* practised
 11 *mark* distinctive characteristic; and with sexual connotation
 12 *deft* dainty
 13 *lusty* large
    sprig an ornament made from a sprig of a plant; or perhaps an ornament made
    in the shape of a sprig; and with sexual connotation

Or else his out of hers, if she be near him.
The love of kindred never yet stuck closer
Than theirs to one another; he that weds her
Marries her uncle's heart too.

Cornets [sound]

WARD   Say you so, sir,
   Then I'll be asked i'th'church to both of them.   20
GUARDIANO
   Fall back, here comes the Duke.
WARD   He brings a gentle-
      woman,
   I should fall forward rather.

      Enter DUKE, BIANCA, FABRITIO, HIPPOLITO, LIVIA,
            MOTHER, ISABELLA, *and* ATTENDANTS

DUKE   Come, Bianca,
   Of purpose sent into the world to show
   Perfection once in woman; I'll believe
   Henceforward they have ev'ry one a soul too,   25
   'Gainst all the uncourteous opinions
   That man's uncivil rudeness ever held of 'em.
   Glory of Florence, light into mine arms!

                        Enter LEANTIO

BIANCA
   Yon comes a grudging man will chide you, sir.
   The storm is now in's heart and would get nearer,   30
   And fall here if it durst; it pours down yonder.
DUKE
   If that be he, the weather shall soon clear.
   List, and I'll tell thee how. [*Whispers to* BIANCA]
LEANTIO [*Aside*]   A-kissing too?
   I see 'tis plain lust now, adultery boldened;
   What will it prove anon, when 'tis stuffed full   35
   Of wine and sweetmeats, being so impudent fasting?
DUKE
   [*To* LEANTIO] We have heard of your good parts, sir,
      which we honour

---

22 *fall forward* i.e. have sex
25 *soul* There is no mention in Genesis 2:7 of God breathing a soul into Eve, as He
   did for Adam; hence, the alleged absence of a soul in woman became a stock
   misogynist insult. The question was hotly debated in the pamphlets concerned
   with the controversy over women; see the Introduction.
28 *light* arrive (a verb). Cf. I.ii.56.
36 *impudent* immodest
37 *parts* qualities

With our embrace and love. [*To* GENTLEMAN] Is not
  the captainship
Of Rouans' citadel, since the late deceased,
Supplied by any yet?
GENTLEMAN   By none, my lord.   40
DUKE
  [*To* LEANTIO] Take it, the place is yours then, and as faith-
    fulness
  And desert grows, our favour shall grow with't:

              [LEANTIO *kneels*]

  Rise now the captain of our fort at Rouans.
LEANTIO
  The service of whole life give your grace thanks.
DUKE
  Come sit, Bianca.
LEANTIO [*Aside*]   This is some good yet,   45
  And more than ev'r I looked for; a fine bit
  To stay a cuckold's stomach. All preferment
  That springs from sin and lust, it shoots up quickly,
  As gardeners' crops do in the rotten'st grounds;
  So is all means raised from base prostitution,   50
  Ev'n like a sallet growing upon a dunghill.
  I'm like a thing that never was yet heard of,
  Half merry and half mad – much like a fellow
  That eats his meat with a good appetite,
  And wears a plague-sore that would fright a country;   55
  Or rather like the barren, hardened ass,
  That feeds on thistles till he bleeds again.
  And such is the condition of my misery.
LIVIA
  Is that your son, widow?
MOTHER   Yes, did your ladyship
  Never know that till now?
LIVIA   No, trust me, did I.   60
  [*Aside*] Nor ever truly felt the power of love
  And pity to a man, till now I knew him.

39, 43 *Rouans* Middleton may have meant Rouens; but in his *Itinerary* (I, Book 2,
p. 148), Fynes Moryson refers to one of the forts at Florence as being in an area
where 'there is a place vulgarly called *le Ruinate*, that is, the ruinous', and the
(ironic) name may have been intended as appropriate for Leantio.
47 *stay* settle; enhance
50 *means* resources
51 *sallet* any green vegetable used in a salad
56 *barren* stupid
59–60 *ladyship / Never* ed. (Ladiship never O)

I have enough to buy me my desires,
And yet to spare; that's one good comfort. [*To* LEANTIO]
   Hark you,
Pray let me speak with you, sir, before you go.   65

LEANTIO
With me, lady? You shall, I am at your service.
[*Aside*] What will she say now, trow, more goodness yet?

WARD
I see her now, I'm sure; the ape's so little,
I shall scarce feel her; I have seen almost
As tall as she sold in the fair for ten pence.   70
See how she simpers it, as if marmalade
Would not melt in her mouth! She might have the
   kindness, i'faith,
To send me a gilded bull from her own trencher,
A ram, a goat, or somewhat to be nibbling.
These women when they come to sweet things once,   75
They forget all their friends, they grow so greedy;
Nay, oftentimes their husbands.

DUKE   Here's a health now,
   gallants,
To the best beauty at this day in Florence.

BIANCA
Whoe'er she be, she shall not go unpledged, sir.

DUKE
Nay, you're excused for this.

BIANCA   Who, I my lord?   80

DUKE
Yes, by the law of Bacchus; plead your benefit,
You are not bound to pledge your own health, lady.

BIANCA
That's a good way, my lord, to keep me dry.

---

68 *ape* a term of endearment

70 *for ten pence* i.e. not worth much at all

71-2 *marmalade ... mouth* Proverbial: 'He looks as if butter would not melt in his
   mouth' (Tilley, B 774).

73 *trencher* platter

73-4 *gilded bull ... ram ... goat* more animal figures in marzipan; cf. the 'colt' at
   III.i.269. All these animals were standard emblems of lechery; they also all wore
   horns, thus suggesting that the Ward will be a cuckold.

77 *health* a toast

81 *Bacchus* god of wine
   plead your benefit claim your exemption from this 'law' (through 'benefit of clergy',
   literate people could claim exemption from the law)

83 *dry* thirsty; lacking sexual moistness (continued in the reference to 'Venus' in the
   next line)

DUKE
Nay, then I will not offend Venus so much,
Let Bacchus seek his 'mends in another court.   85
Here's to thyself, Bianca. [*He drinks*]
BIANCA   Nothing comes
More welcome to that name than your grace. [*She drinks*]
LEANTIO [*Aside*]   So, so;
Here stands the poor thief now that stole the treasure,
And he's not thought on. Ours is near kin now
To a twin misery born into the world: 90
First the hard-conscienced worldling, he hoards wealth
    up;
Then comes the next, and he feasts all upon't;
One's damned for getting, th'other for spending on't.
Oh equal justice, thou hast met my sin
With a full weight; I'm rightly now oppressed,   95
All her friends' heavy hearts lie in my breast.
DUKE
Methinks there is no spirit amongst us, gallants,
But what divinely sparkles from the eyes
Of bright Bianca; we sat all in darkness,
But for that splendour. Who was't told us lately   100
Of a match-making rite, a marriage-tender?
GUARDIANO
'Twas I, my Lord.
DUKE   'Twas you indeed. Where is she?
GUARDIANO
This is the gentlewoman.
FABRITIO   My lord, my daughter.
DUKE
Why, here's some stirring yet.
FABRITIO   She's a dear child to me.
DUKE
That must needs be; you say she is your daughter.   105
FABRITIO
Nay, my good lord, dear to my purse, I mean,
Beside my person; I nev'r reckoned that.
She has the full qualities of a gentlewoman;
I have brought her up to music, dancing, what not,
That may commend her sex and stir her husband.   110

---

85 *'mends* legal remedies
96 i.e. I am now suffering as much as her friends from whom I 'stole' (l. 88) her
101 *marriage-tender* formal offer of marriage
104 *some stirring yet* i.e. here's some excitement; also with sexual connotation (cf. 'stir', l. 110)

DUKE
  And which is he now?
GUARDIANO   This young heir, my lord.
DUKE
  What is he brought up to?
HIPPOLITO [*Aside*]   To cat and trap.
GUARDIANO
  My lord, he's a great ward, wealthy, but simple;
  His parts consist in acres.
DUKE   Oh, wise-acres!
GUARDIANO
  Y'have spoke him in a word, sir.
BIANCA   'Las, poor gentle-   115
    woman,
  She's ill bestead, unless sh'as dealt the wiselier
  And laid in more provision for her youth:
  Fools will not keep in summer.
LEANTIO [*Aside*]   No, nor such wives
  From whores in winter.
DUKE   Yea, the voice too, sir?
FABRITIO
  Ay, and a sweet breast too, my lord, I hope,   120
  Or I have cast away my money wisely;
  She took her pricksong earlier, my lord,
  Than any of her kindred ever did.
  A rare child, though I say't, but I'd not have
  The baggage hear so much; 'twould make her swell
    straight,   125
  And maids of all things must not be puffed up.
DUKE
  Let's turn us to a better banquet, then,
  For music bids the soul of man to a feast,
  And that's indeed a noble entertainment,

112 *cat and trap* Cf. I.ii.87 s.d.n.
114 *parts* qualities
116 *bestead* situated
118–19 *Fools ... winter* 'Fools' (= delicacy, trifle; cf. I.ii.116n.) will go bad in the
    heat of the summer, while wives will go bad in winter (i.e. turn into a whore =
    hoar, or hoarfrost).
120 *breast* singing voice; bosom. Fabritio unwittingly praises Isabella's musical talents
    in sexual double meanings (see next two notes).
122 *pricksong* written music, 'pricked' into the paper. The obvious sexual pun on
    'prick' leads to 'swell' (l. 125) and 'puffed up' (l. 126) = proud; pregnant.
125 *baggage* a demeaning term for a young woman. Cf. Juliet's father: 'Out, you
    baggage!' (*Romeo and Juliet* III.v.156).
128 *of man* ed. (of a man O)

Worthy Bianca's self. [*To her*] You shall perceive,
  beauty,   130
Our Florentine damsels are not brought up idly.
BIANCA
They are wiser of themselves, it seems, my lord,
And can take gifts when goodness offers 'em.

                    Music

LEANTIO
[*Aside*] True, and damnation has taught you that
  wisdom,
You can take gifts, too. Oh that music mocks me!   135
LIVIA
[*Aside*] I am as dumb to any language now
But love's, as one that never learned to speak.
I am not yet so old but he may think of me;
My own fault, I have been idle a long time;
But I'll begin the week and paint tomorrow,   140
So follow my true labour day by day.
I never thrived so well as when I used it.
[ISABELLA *sings*]

                    Song
What harder chance can fall to woman,
Who was born to cleave to some man,
Than to bestow her time, youth, beauty,   145
Life's observance, honour, duty,
On a thing for no use good,
But to make physic work, or blood
Force fresh in an old lady's cheek?
She that would be   150
Mother of fools, let her compound with me.
WARD
Here's a tune indeed! Pish, I had rather hear one ballad
sung i'th'nose now, of the lamentable drowning of fat
sheep and oxen, than all these simpering tunes played
upon cats' guts and sung by little kitlings.   155

---

140 *paint* use cosmetics, a practice invariably condemned on moral grounds. Cf.
  Hamlet's 'let her paint an inch thick' (*Hamlet* V.i.193).
143–55 The Ward's commentary may be spoken simultaneously with the song, as O
  prints them side by side.
148 *make physic work* make a medicine work through mild excitement – an ironic
  comment on the Ward's power to stimulate sexually. 'Physic' may also = laxative.
148–9 *blood / Force* ed. (blood force O)
149 *fresh in* ed. (fresh / In O)
149–50 *cheek? / She* ed. (cheek, she O)
151 *compound with* join or agree with
155 *kitlings* little cats; whores

FABRITIO
  How like you her breast now, my lord?
BIANCA [*Aside to* DUKE]   Her breast?
  He talks as if his daughter had given suck
  Before she were married, as her betters have;
  The next he praises, sure, will be her nipples.
DUKE
  [*Aside to her*] Methinks now, such a voice to such a
      husband   160
  Is like a jewel of unvalued worth
  Hung at a fool's ear.
FABRITIO   May it please your grace
  To give her leave to show another quality?
DUKE
  Marry, as many good ones as you will, sir,
  The more the better welcome.
LEANTIO [*Aside*]   But the less   165
  The better practised. That soul's black indeed
  That cannot commend virtue; but who keeps it?
  The extortioner will say to a sick beggar,
  Heaven comfort thee, though he give none himself.
  This good is common.
FABRITIO   Will it please you now, sir,   170
  To entreat your ward to take her by the hand,
  And lead her in a dance before the Duke?
GUARDIANO
  That will I, sir, 'tis needful. Hark you, nephew.
FABRITIO
  Nay, you shall see, young heir, what y'have for your
      money,
  Without fraud or imposture.
WARD   Dance with her!   175
  Not I, sweet guardianer, do not urge my heart to't,
  'Tis clean against my blood; dance with a stranger!
  Let whoso will do't, I'll not begin first with her.

---

156 *Her breast?* Bianca's reaction suggests the term 'breast' for 'voice' was an odd,
    affected usage.
160 *to* compared to
161 *unvalued* priceless
172–99 A dance was a traditional emblem of harmony, and often associated with
    weddings, but below the surface harmony here is a complex sexual intrigue.
177 *blood* inclination
178 *whoso* ed. (who's O)

HIPPOLITO
   [*Aside*] No, fear't not, fool, sh'as took a better order.
GUARDIANO
   Why, who shall take her then?
WARD   Some other gentleman.   180
   Look, there's her uncle, a fine-timbered reveller –
   Perhaps he knows the manner of her dancing, too;
   I'll have him do't before me. I have sworn, guardianer;
   Then may I learn the better.
GUARDIANO   Thou'lt be an ass still.
WARD
   Ay, all that, uncle, shall not fool me out.   185
   Pish, I stick closer to myself than so.
GUARDIANO
   [*To* HIPPOLITO] I must entreat you, sir, to take your
      niece
   And dance with her; my ward's a little wilful,
   He would have you show him the way.
HIPPOLITO   Me, sir?
   He shall command it at all hours, pray tell him so.   190
GUARDIANO
   I thank you for him, he has not wit himself, sir.
HIPPOLITO
   [*To* ISABELLA] Come, my life's peace. [*Aside*] I have a
      strange office on't here.
   'Tis some man's luck to keep the joys he likes
   Concealed for his own bosom, but my fortune
   To set 'em out now, for another's liking –   195
   Like the mad misery of necessitous man,
   That parts from his good horse with many praises,
   And goes on foot himself. Need must be obeyed
   In ev'ry action, it mars man and maid.

Music. A dance [*by* HIPPOLITO *and* ISABELLA], *making honours
to the* DUKE *and curtsy to themselves, both before and after*

DUKE
   Signor Fabritio, y'are a happy father,   200
   Your cares and pains are fortunate; you see
   Your cost bears noble fruits. Hippolito, thanks.

179 *a better order* i.e. she has made a better arrangement, by taking Hippolito before
    the Ward
180 *take her* take for the dance; take sexually
181 *fine-timbered* well-built
185 *fool me out* i.e. make me change my mind
192 *office* duty
198 *Need* necessity   199 s.d.1 *honours* bows

FABRITIO
　Here's some amends for all my charges yet:
　She wins both prick and praise where'er she comes.
DUKE
　How lik'st, Bianca?
BIANCA　　　　　　　All things well, my lord,　　　　　205
　But this poor gentlewoman's fortune, that's the worst.
DUKE
　There is no doubt, Bianca, she'll find leisure
　To make that good enough; he's rich and simple.
BIANCA
　She has the better hope o'th'upper hand, indeed,
　Which women strive for most.
GUARDIANO [To WARD]　　　　Do't when I bid you, sir.　210
WARD
　I'll venture but a hornpipe with her, guardianer,
　Or some such married man's dance.
GUARDIANO　　　　　　　　　　Well, venture
　　something, sir.
WARD
　I have rhyme for what I do.
GUARDIANO [Aside]　　　　But little reason, I think.
WARD
　Plain men dance the measures, the cinquepace the gay;
　Cuckolds dance the hornpipe, and farmers dance the
　　hay;　　　　　　　　　　　　　　　　　　　215
　Your soldiers dance the round, and maidens that grow
　　big;
　Your drunkards, the canaries; your whore and bawd, the
　　jig.
　Here's your eight kind of dancers, he that finds the ninth,
　let him pay the minstrels.

204 *prick and praise* i.e. highest praise. The 'prick' was the mark in the centre of an
　archery target; there is also an obvious sexual connotation, to which Fabritio may
　be oblivious.
211 *hornpipe* a vigorous dance; 'horn' = cuckold and 'pipe' = phallus, hence the
　suitability of this dance for a 'married man' (l. 212)
212 *Well* ed. (we'll O)
214 *measures* a stately dance
　cinquepace galliard (a lively French dance)
215 *hay* country dance
216 *round* circling dance; also, the watch kept by soldiers
217 *Your ... your* ed. (you ... you O)
　canaries lively dance thought to have come from the Canary Islands; also a sweet
　wine from the Canary Islands
　jig lively, rapid dance; associated with lewdness

DUKE

Oh here he appears once in his own person!   220
I thought he would have married her by attorney,
And lain with her so too.

BIANCA   Nay, my kind lord,
There's very seldom any found so foolish
To give away his part there.

LEANTIO [*Aside*]   Bitter scoff!
Yet I must do't; with what a cruel pride   225
The glory of her sin strikes by my afflictions!

Music. [The] WARD *and* ISABELLA *dance*;
he ridiculously imitates HIPPOLITO

DUKE

This thing will make shift, sirs, to make a husband,
For aught I see in him; how thinks't, Bianca?

BIANCA

'Faith, an ill-favoured shift, my lord. Methinks
If he would take some voyage when he's married,   230
Dangerous, or long enough, and scarce be seen
Once in nine year together, a wife then
Might make indifferent shift to be content with him.

DUKE

A kiss! [*Kisses* BIANCA] That wit deserves to be made
    much on.
Come, our caroche.

GUARDIANO   Stands ready for your grace.   235

DUKE

My thanks to all your loves. Come, fair Bianca,
We have took special care of you, and provided
Your lodging near us now.

BIANCA   Your love is great, my lord.

DUKE

Once more our thanks to all.

OMNES   All blest honours guard
    you.

Cornets flourish

Exe[unt] all but LEANTIO *and* LIVIA

221 *by attorney* by proxy
226 *glory* boastfulness
    strikes by thrusts aside
229 *shift* attempt
235 *caroche* a stately coach

LEANTIO

    [*Aside*] Oh hast thou left me then, Bianca, utterly!   240
    Bianca! Now I miss thee. Oh return,
    And save the faith of woman! I nev'r felt
    The loss of thee till now; 'tis an affliction
    Of greater weight than youth was made to bear,
    As if a punishment of after-life   245
    Were fall'n upon man here; so new it is
    To flesh and blood, so strange, so insupportable
    A torment, ev'n mistook, as if a body
    Whose death were drowning must needs therefore
        suffer it
    In scalding oil.

LIVIA   Sweet sir!

LEANTIO [*Aside*]   As long as mine eye saw thee,   250
    I half enjoyed thee.

LIVIA   Sir?

LEANTIO [*Aside*]   Canst thou forget
    The dear pains my love took, how it has watched
    Whole nights together in all weathers for thee,
    Yet stood in heart more merry than the tempests
    That sung about mine ears, like dangerous flatterers   255
    That can set all their mischief to sweet tunes;
    And then received thee from thy father's window
    Into these arms at midnight, when we embraced
    As if we had been statues only made for't,
    To show art's life, so silent were our comforts,   260
    And kissed as if our lips had grown together!

LIVIA

    [*Aside*] This makes me madder to enjoy him now.

LEANTIO

    [*Aside*] Canst thou forget all this? And better joys
    That we met after this, which then new kisses
    Took pride to praise?

LIVIA [*Aside*]   I shall grow madder yet. [*To him*]
    Sir!   265

LEANTIO

    [*Aside*] This cannot be but of some close bawd's working.
    [*To her*] Cry mercy, lady. What would you say to me?
    My sorrow makes me so unmannerly,
    So comfort bless me, I had quite forgot you.

248 *A torment, ev'n mistook* mistaken torment
259 *only made for't* only made for embracing
260 *show art's life* to show how lifelike the artwork is
266 *close* secret

LIVIA

Nothing but, ev'n in pity to that passion,   270
Would give your grief good counsel.

LEANTIO   Marry, and
    welcome, lady;
It never could come better.

LIVIA   Then first, sir,
To make away all your good thoughts at once of her,
Know most assuredly she is a strumpet.

LEANTIO

Ha! 'Most assuredly'! Speak not a thing   275
So vilde so certainly, leave it more doubtful.

LIVIA

Then I must leave all truth, and spare my knowledge,
A sin which I too lately found and wept for.

LEANTIO

Found you it?

LIVIA   Ay, with wet eyes.

LEANTIO   Oh perjurious friend-
    ship!

LIVIA

You missed your fortunes when you met with her, sir.   280
Young gentlemen that only love for beauty,
They love not wisely; such a marriage rather
Proves the destruction of affection –
It brings on want, and want's the key of whoredom.
I think y'had small means with her.

LEANTIO   Oh not any, lady.   285

LIVIA

Alas, poor gentleman, what meant'st thou, sir,
Quite to undo thyself with thine own kind heart?
Thou art too good and pitiful to woman.
Marry, sir, thank thy stars for this blest fortune
That rids the summer of thy youth so well   290
From many beggars that had lain a-sunning
In thy beams only else, till thou hadst wasted
The whole days of thy life in heat and labour.
What would you say now to a creature found
As pitiful to you, and as it were   295
Ev'n sent on purpose from the whole sex general,
To requite all that kindness you have shown to't?

276 *vilde* vile
285 *small means* i.e. she had no real dowry
296 *sex general* all women

LEANTIO
  What's that, madam?
LIVIA   Nay, a gentlewoman, and one able
  To reward good things, ay, and bears a conscience to't.
  Could'st thou love such a one, that – blow all fortunes –   300
  Would never see thee want?
  Nay more, maintain thee to thine enemy's envy?
  And shalt not spend a care for't, stir a thought,
  Nor break a sleep, unless love's music waked thee;
  No storm of fortune should. Look upon me,   305
  And know that woman.
LEANTIO   Oh my life's wealth, Bianca!
LIVIA
  Still with her name? Will nothing wear it out?
  That deep sigh went but for a strumpet, sir.
LEANTIO
  It can go for no other that loves me.
LIVIA
  [Aside] He's vexed in mind; I came too soon to him;   310
  Where's my discretion now, my skill, my judgement?
  I'm cunning in all arts but my own love.
  'Tis as unseasonable to tempt him now
  So soon, as a widow to be courted
  Following her husband's corse, or to make bargain   315
  By the grave-side, and take a young man there:
  Her strange departure stands like a hearse yet
  Before his eyes, which time will take down shortly.
                                                        Exit

LEANTIO
  Is she my wife till death, yet no more mine?
  That's a hard measure. Then what's marriage good for?   320
  Methinks by right I should not now be living,
  And then 'twere all well. What a happiness
  Had I been made of, had I never seen her;
  For nothing makes man's loss grievous to him
  But knowledge of the worth of what he loses;   325
  For what he never had, he never misses.
  She's gone for ever, utterly; there is
  As much redemption of a soul from Hell,

300 *blow all fortunes* i.e. come what may
303 *And shalt* and you shall
314–15 *widow . . . corse* As Richard courted Lady Anne in the presence of her father-
    in-law's corpse in *Richard III*.
317 *strange* like a stranger; not yet familiar
    hearse a wooden structure erected over the coffin for a certain period of time
327–8 *there . . . Hell* Proverbial: 'There is no Redemption from hell' (Tilley, R 60).

As a fair woman's body from his palace.
Why should my love last longer than her truth?   330
What is there good in woman to be loved
When only that which makes her so has left her?
I cannot love her now, but I must like
Her sin, and my own shame too, and be guilty
Of law's breach with her, and mine own abusing;   335
All which were monstrous. Then my safest course,
For health of mind and body, is to turn
My heart, and hate her, most extremely hate her;
I have no other way. Those virtuous powers
Which were chaste witnesses of both our troths,   340
Can witness she breaks first – and I'm rewarded
With captainship o'th'fort! A place of credit,
I must confess, but poor; my factorship
Shall not exchange means with't. He that died last in't,
He was no drunkard, yet he died a beggar   345
For all his thrift. Besides, the place not fits me:
It suits my resolution, not my breeding.

Enter LIVIA

LIVIA
    [*Aside*] I have tried all ways I can, and have not power
    To keep from sight of him. [*To him*] How are you now,
        sir?
LEANTIO
    I feel a better ease, madam.
LIVIA   Thanks to blessedness!   350
    You will do well, I warrant you, fear it not, sir.
    Join but your own good will to't; he's not wise
    That loves his pain or sickness, or grows fond
    Of a disease whose property is to vex him
    And spitefully drink his blood up. Out upon't, sir,   355
    Youth knows no greater loss. I pray let's walk, sir.
    You never saw the beauty of my house yet,
    Nor how abundantly fortune has blessed me
    In worldly treasure; trust me, I have enough, sir,
    To make my friend a rich man in my life,   360

330 *truth* faithfulness
333 *but* unless
335 *law's breach* i.e. adultery
342–4 *place . . . with't* i.e. the captainship is an honour, but it does not even pay as
    much as his factorship
347 *my resolution, not my breeding* my courage, not my low birth
355 *drink his blood up* Unrequited love was widely believed to dry up the blood.
360 *friend* lover. See II.i.153n.

A great man at my death; yourself will say so.
If you want anything and spare to speak,
Troth, I'll condemn you for a wilful man, sir.

LEANTIO
Why sure, this can be but the flattery of some dream.

LIVIA
Now by this kiss, my love, my soul and riches,   365
'Tis all true substance. [*Kisses him*]
Come, you shall see my wealth, take what you list;
The gallanter you go, the more you please me.
I will allow you, too, your page and footman,
Your race-horses, or any various pleasure   370
Exercised youth delights in. But to me
Only, sir, wear your heart of constant stuff;
Do but you love enough, I'll give enough.

LEANTIO
Troth then, I'll love enough and take enough.

LIVIA
Then we are both pleased enough.   375

Exeunt

Act III, Scene iii

Enter GUARDIANO *and* ISABELLA *at one door,*
and the WARD *and* SORDIDO *at another*

GUARDIANO
Now, nephew, here's the gentlewoman again.

WARD
Mass, here she's come again; mark her now, Sordido.

GUARDIANO
This is the maid my love and care has chose
Out for your wife, and so I tender her to you;
Yourself has been eye-witness of some qualities   5
That speak a courtly breeding, and are costly.
I bring you both to talk together now,
'Tis time you grew familiar in your tongues;
Tomorrow you join hands, and one ring ties you,
And one bed holds you – if you like the choice.   10
Her father and her friends are i'th'next room,
And stay to see the contract ere they part;
Therefore dispatch, good Ward, be sweet and short.

372 *constant stuff* i.e. of one colour; figuratively, to be faithful
  12 *contract* marriage contract

Like her or like her not, there's but two ways;
And one your body, th'other your purse pays.   15
WARD
I warrant you, guardianer, I'll not stand all day
      thrumming,
But quickly shoot my bolt at your next coming.
GUARDIANO
Well said! Good fortune to your birding then.   [*Exit*]
WARD
I never missed mark yet.
SORDIDO
Troth, I think, master, if the truth were known,   20
You never shot at any but the kitchen-wench,
And that was a she-woodcock, a mere innocent,
That was oft lost, and cried at eight and twenty.
WARD
No more of that meat, Sordido, here's eggs o'th'spit
      now,
We must turn gingerly. Draw out the catalogue   25
Of all the faults of women.
SORDIDO
How, all the faults! Have you so little reason to think so
much paper will lie in my breeches? Why, ten carts will
not carry it, if you set down but the bawds. All the faults?
Pray let's be content with a few of 'em; and if they were   30
less, you would find 'em enough, I warrant you. Look
you, sir.
ISABELLA
[*Aside*] But that I have th'advantage of the fool
As much as woman's heart can wish and joy at,
What an infernal torment 'twere to be   35

14–15 *two . . . pays* The Ward has two choices, both of which require him to 'pay':
   either marry (giving his body), or pay a fine to his guardian (cf. I.ii.3n.).
16 *thrumming* playing a musical instrument idly; copulating
17 *shoot my bolt* give my decision; ejaculate. Proverbial: 'A Fool's bolt is soon shot'
   (Tilley, F 515); the 'bolt' or bird-bolt was an arrow used for fowling (cf. 'birding',
   l. 18), and was also frequently associated with Cupid.
18 *birding* fowling; wenching
19 *mark* archery target; figuratively, female genitals
22 *she-woodcock* a simpleton ('innocent' = half-wit). The woodcock was proverbially
   an easy bird to capture.
23 *cried* i.e. like a lost child announced by the town-crier
24 *eggs o'th'spit* i.e. delicate business
28 *carts* Carting, or carrying criminals (especially women) through the streets in a
   cart, was a common legal punishment.

Thus bought and sold, and turned and pried into; when,
    alas,
The worst bit is too good for him! And the comfort is,
H'as but a cater's place on't, and provides
All for another's table; yet how curious
The ass is, like some nice professor on't,   40
That buys up all the daintiest food i'th'markets,
And seldom licks his lips after a taste on't!

SORDIDO
Now to her, now y'have scanned all her parts over.

WARD
But at what end shall I begin now, Sordido?

SORDIDO
Oh ever at a woman's lip, while you live, sir; do you ask   45
that question?

WARD
Methinks, Sordido, sh'as but a crabbed face to begin
with.

SORDIDO
A crabbed face? That will save money.

WARD
How! Save money, Sordido?   50

SORDIDO
Ay, sir, for having a crabbed face of her own, she'll eat
the less verjuice with her mutton; 'twill save verjuice at
year's end, sir.

WARD
Nay, and your jests begin to be saucy once, I'll make you   55
eat your meat without mustard.

SORDIDO
And that in some kind is a punishment.

WARD
Gentlewoman, they say 'tis your pleasure to be my wife,
and you shall know shortly whether it be mine or no, to
be your husband; and thereupon thus I first enter upon
you. [*Kisses her*] Oh most delicious scent! Methinks it   60
tasted as if a man had stepped into a comfit-maker's shop
to let a cart go by, all the while I kissed her. It is reported,

38 *cater's* the person who buys the 'cates', or provisions, for a household
39 *curious* fastidious
40 *nice professor* pedantic expert (one who 'professes' knowledge)
44 *what* ed. (*not in* O)
51 *crabbed* punning on 'crab' = crab-apple
52 *verjuice* sour juice or puree made from crab-apples, used as a condiment
54 *and* if
61 *comfit-maker's shop* i.e. a sweet-smelling place; a comfit-maker = confectioner

gentlewoman, you'll run mad for me, if you have me not.

ISABELLA

I should be in great danger of my wits, sir,
For being so forward, [*Aside*] should this ass kick
   backward now!   65

WARD

Alas, poor soul! And is that hair your own?

ISABELLA

Mine own? Yes sure, sir, I owe nothing for't.

WARD

'Tis a good hearing; I shall have the less to pay when I
have married you.
[*To* SORDIDO] Look, does her eyes stand well?

SORDIDO   They
   cannot stand better   70
Than in her head, I think; where would you have them?
And for her nose, 'tis of a very good last.

WARD

I have known as good as that has not lasted a year,
though.

SORDIDO

That's in the using of a thing; will not any strong bridge   75
fall down in time, if we do nothing but beat at the bottom?
A nose of buff would not last always, sir, especially if
it came in to th'camp once.

WARD

But Sordido, how shall we do to make her laugh, that I
may see what teeth she has? For I'll not bate her a tooth,   80
nor take a black one into th'bargain.

SORDIDO

Why, do but you fall in talk with her, you cannot choose
but one time or other make her laugh, sir.

WARD

It shall go hard, but I will. [*To her*] Pray what qualities

---

66 *hair your own?* Loss of hair was one symptom of venereal disease; wearing an
   elaborate wig was also a sign of vanity and affectation in women. The boy-actor
   playing Isabella, in a final irony, was of course wearing a wig.

68 *good hearing* good to hear

70 *does her eyes stand well?* are her eyes well-placed?

72 *last* shape (the cobbler's 'last' stretches a shoe to its correct shape)

72–8 *last . . . once* This dialogue on the shape of her nose again alludes to venereal
   disease: one symptom was the collapse of the nose's structure.

77 *buff* strong leather (used for military uniforms), hence tough

78 *camp* military camp. A 'camp-follower' = whore; a 'camp' was associated with
   venereal disease, which would destroy even a 'nose of buff'.

80 *bate* accept less than the full number

have you beside singing and dancing? Can you play at   85
shittlecock, forsooth?

ISABELLA
Ay, and at stool-ball too, sir; I have great luck at it.

WARD
Why, can you catch a ball well?

ISABELLA
I have catched two in my lap at one game.

WARD
What, have you, woman? I must have you learn   90
To play at trap too, then y'are full and whole.

ISABELLA
Anything that you please to bring me up to
I shall take pains to practise.

WARD
[Aside to SORDIDO] 'Twill not do, Sordido, we shall never
get her mouth opened wide enough.   95

SORDIDO
No, sir? That's strange! Then here's a trick for your
learning.

　　　　　He yawns[; ISABELLA yawns also,
　　　　　　　but covers her mouth]

Look now, look now; quick, quick there!

WARD
Pox of that scurvy, mannerly trick with handkerchief;
It hindered me a little, but I am satisfied.   100
When a fair woman gapes and stops her mouth so,
It shows like a cloth-stopple in a cream-pot.
I have fair hope of her teeth now, Sordido.

SORDIDO
Why, then y'have all well, sir; for aught I see
She's right and straight enough, now as she stands. 105
They'll commonly lie crooked, that's no matter.
Wise gamesters never find fault with that, let 'em lie
　　still so.

87 *stool-ball* a game resembling cricket, in which the wicket was a stool; one player
　defended it from a ball thrown by another. Like the games of 'shittlecock' (l. 86;
　cf. II.ii.79 s.d.n.) and tip-cat ('trap', l. 91; cf. I.ii.87 s.d.n.), the game of stool-
　ball becomes a metaphor for sexual intercourse, reflected in the bawdy dialogue
　in ll. 87–93. The excretory pun is also picked up in this phrase.
91–2 *full and whole ... bring me up to* with sexual connotation
102 *cloth-stopple* stopper of cloth
106 *lie crooked* They are not 'straight' when they lie (sexually) down; they tell crooked
　lies.
107 *gamesters* sexual sportsmen
　gamesters never ed. (Gamesters / Never O)

WARD

I'd fain mark how she goes, and then I have all. For of
all creatures I cannot abide a splay-footed woman, she's
an unlucky thing to meet in a morning; her heels keep   110
together so, as if she were beginning an Irish dance still,
and the wriggling of her bum, playing the tune to't. But
I have bethought a cleanly shift to find it: dab down as
you see me, and peep of one side when her back's toward
you; I'll show you the way.   115

SORDIDO

And you shall find me apt enough to peeping,
I have been one of them has seen mad sights
Under your scaffolds.

WARD [*To* ISABELLA]   Will it please you walk, forsooth,
A turn or two by yourself? You are so pleasing to me,
I take delight to view you on both sides.   120

ISABELLA

I shall be glad to fetch a walk to your love, sir;
'Twill get affection a good stomach, sir.
[*Aside*] Which I had need have, to fall to such coarse
victuals.

> [*She walks about while they
> duck down to look up her dress*]

WARD

Now go thy ways for a clean-treading wench,
As ever man in modesty peeped under.   125

SORDIDO

I see the sweetest sight to please my master!
Never went Frenchman righter upon ropes
Than she on Florentine rushes.

WARD [*To* ISABELLA]   'Tis enough, forsooth.

108 *goes* walks
109 *splay-footed* feet turned out while walking (supposedly a sign to know a witch by)
111 *Irish dance* begun with one heel touching the other foot's instep, as described here
     still always
112 *the ... the* ed. (he ... the O)
113 *cleanly shift* neat trick
     dab down duck down
118 *scaffolds* raised areas for spectators
122 *stomach* i.e. sexual appetite
124 *clean-treading* straight-walking; also, 'tread' = sexual intercourse
127 *Frenchman ... ropes* walking on a tightrope, especially by visiting French performers. Cf. Jonson's *Epicoene*: 'the Frenchman that walks upon ropes' (II.ii.52–3).
128 *rushes* used as a floor-covering

ISABELLA

   And how do you like me now, sir?

WARD   'Faith, so well,

   I never mean to part with thee, sweetheart,   130

   Under some sixteen children, and all boys.

ISABELLA

   You'll be at simple pains, if you prove kind,

   And breed 'em all in your teeth.

WARD   Nay, by my faith,

   What serves your belly for? 'Twould make my cheeks

   Look like blown bagpipes.

Enter GUARDIANO

GUARDIANO   How now, ward and nephew,   135

   Gentlewoman and niece! Speak, is it so or not?

WARD

   'Tis so, we are both agreed, sir.

GUARDIANO   In to your kindred, then;

   There's friends, and wine, and music, waits to welcome

      you.

WARD

   Then I'll be drunk for joy.

SORDIDO   And I for company,

   I cannot break my nose in a better action.   140

Exeunt

129–30 *well,* / *I* ed. (well, I O)

132 *simple pains* great pains; the pains appropriate to a fool (= 'simple')
    kind in your natural character

133 *teeth* A sympathetic toothache was believed to be a common psychosomatic illness
    in a husband whose wife was pregnant.

133–4 *faith,* / *What* ed. (Faith, what O)

134–5 *cheeks* / *Look* ed. (cheeks look O)

140 *break . . . action* i.e. suffer in a better cause

Act IV, Scene i

Enter BIANCA *attended by two* LADIES

BIANCA
How goes your watches, ladies? What's o'clock now?
1 LADY
By mine, full nine.
2 LADY   By mine, a quarter past.
1 LADY
I set mine by St Mark's.
2 LADY   St Antony's, they say,
Goes truer.
1 LADY   That's but your opinion, madam,
Because you love a gentleman o'th'name.   5
2 LADY
He's a true gentleman, then.
1 LADY   So may he be
That comes to me tonight, for aught you know.
BIANCA
I'll end this strife straight. I set mine by the sun;
I love to set by th'best, one shall not then
Be troubled to set often.
2 LADY   You do wisely in't.   10
BIANCA
If I should set my watch as some girls do
By ev'ry clock i'th'town, 'twould nev'r go true;
And too much turning of the dial's point,
Or tampering with the spring, might in small time
Spoil the whole work too. Here it wants of nine now.   15
1 LADY
It does indeed, forsooth; mine's nearest truth yet.
2 LADY
Yet I have found her lying with an advocate, which
showed

1–18 This dialogue about clocks is also a debate about sexual fidelity. Watches, like women, were notoriously unreliable, according to this misogynist analogy, but Bianca claims an ironic constancy because she sets her watch 'by the sun' (l. 8), i.e. the Duke. The equation woman = clock occurs in several plays of the period – Dekker's *The Honest Whore, Part II* (III.i), Jonson's *Epicoene* (IV.ii) and Middleton's *A Mad World, My Masters* (IV.i), among others. Cf. Shakespeare's *Love's Labour's Lost*: 'A woman, that is like a German clock, / Still a-repairing, ever out of frame, / And never going aright' (III.i.188–90).

3 *St Mark's* church in Florence. Cf. I.iii.85n.

3–4 *say,* / *Goes* ed. (say goes O)

13–14 *dial's point ... spring* i.e. male and female genitals

17 *advocate* An advocate 'lies' professionally; hence both are 'false'.

Like two false clocks together in one parish.

BIANCA
So now I thank you, ladies, I desire
A while to be alone.

1 LADY   And I am nobody,   20
Methinks, unless I have one or other with me.
'Faith, my desire and hers will nev'r be sisters.

Exit LADIES

BIANCA
How strangely woman's fortune comes about!
This was the farthest way to come to me,
All would have judged, that knew me born in Venice   25
And there with many jealous eyes brought up,
That never thought they had me sure enough
But when they were upon me; yet my hap
To meet it here, so far off from my birthplace,
My friends or kindred. 'Tis not good, in sadness,   30
To keep a maid so strict in her young days;
Restraint breeds wandering thoughts, as many fasting
        days
A great desire to see flesh stirring again.
I'll nev'r use any girl of mine so strictly;
Howev'r they're kept, their fortunes find 'em out –   35
I see't in me. If they be got in court,
I'll never forbid 'em the country, nor the court,
Though they be born i'th'country. They will come to't,
And fetch their falls a thousand mile about,
Where one would little think on't.   40

Enter LEANTIO

LEANTIO
[*Aside*] I long to see how my despiser looks,
Now she's come here to court. These are her lodgings;
She's simply now advanced. I took her out
Of no such window, I remember, first;

---

24 *the farthest way* i.e. the most unlikely fate
30 *in sadness* seriously
31–4 *keep . . . strictly* a conventional idea. Cf. Webster's *The White Devil*: 'women are
    more willingly and more gloriously chaste, when they are least restrained of their
    liberty' (I.ii.90–1).
32–3 *fasting . . . stirring* After 1608, laws prohibiting the eating of meat during Lent
    were more strictly enforced; 'stirring' and 'flesh' also have sexual connotations.
36 *got* begotten
39 *fetch . . . about* go a thousand miles out of their way to fall into sin
40 s.d. As Bianca's reaction at l. 46 indicates, Leantio enters richly dressed.
43 *simply* absolutely

That was a great deal lower, and less carved.   45
BIANCA

  [*Aside*] How now? What silkworm's this, i'th'name of
    pride?
  What, is it he?
LEANTIO   A bow i'th'ham to your greatness;
  You must have now three legs, I take it, must you not?
BIANCA

  Then I must take another, I shall want else
  The service I should have; you have but two there.   50
LEANTIO

  Y'are richly placed.
BIANCA   Methinks y'are wondrous brave, sir.
LEANTIO

  A sumptuous lodging!
BIANCA   Y'ave an excellent suit there.
LEANTIO

  A chair of velvet!
BIANCA   Is your cloak lined through, sir?
LEANTIO

  Y'are very stately here.
BIANCA   'Faith, something proud, sir.
LEANTIO

  Stay, stay, let's see your cloth-of-silver slippers.   55
BIANCA

  Who's your shoemaker? H'as made you a neat boot.
LEANTIO

  Will you have a pair? The Duke will lend you spurs.
BIANCA

  Yes, when I ride.
LEANTIO   'Tis a brave life you lead.
BIANCA

  I could nev'r see you in such good clothes

---

46 *silkworm* dressed in silk, i.e. a fancy dresser
48–50 *three legs . . . service* three bows; but with sexual insinuation 'leg' = penis. The
    bawdy dialogue continues with 'service' = deference; sexual satisfaction.
49 *want* lack
51 *brave* well-dressed
53 *lined through* with a lining throughout (a sign of wealth)
55 *cloth-of-silver* cloth with silver threads interwoven (another sign of ostentatious
    wealth)
57 *pair? The* ed. (pair, / The O)
57–8 *lend . . . ride* lend you assistance. Bianca also takes up the sexual connotation
    in her response in l. 58, where 'ride' = ride a horse; have sexual intercourse.
59 *you in* ed. (you / In O)
59–60 *clothes / In* ed. (clothes in O)

In my time.
LEANTIO   In your time?
BIANCA   Sure, I think, sir,   60
We both thrive best asunder.
LEANTIO   Y'are a whore!
BIANCA
Fear nothing, sir.
LEANTIO   An impudent, spiteful strumpet!
BIANCA
Oh sir, you give me thanks for your captainship;
I thought you had forgot all your good manners.
LEANTIO
And to spite thee as much, look there, there read!   65

[*Gives her a letter*]

Vex, gnaw! Thou shalt find there I am not love-starved.
The world was never yet so cold or pitiless
But there was ever still more charity found out
Than at one proud fool's door; and 'twere hard, 'faith,
If I could not pass that. Read to thy shame, there;   70
A cheerful and a beauteous benefactor too,
As ev'r erected the good works of love.
BIANCA   Lady Livia!
[*Aside*] Is't possible? Her worship was my pandress.
She dote, and send and give, and all to him!
Why, here's a bawd plagued home. [*To him*] Y'are
    simply happy, sir,   75
Yet I'll not envy you.
LEANTIO   No, court-saint, not thou!
You keep some friend of a new fashion;
There's no harm in your devil, he's a suckling,
But he will breed teeth shortly, will he not?
BIANCA
Take heed you play not then too long with him.   80
LEANTIO
Yes, and the great one too. I shall find time
To play a hot religious bout with some of you,
And perhaps drive you and your course of sins

70 *pass that* pass by; surpass
72 *as ever* established charitable acts; as ever sexually aroused one
75 *bawd plagued home* punished with the same 'plague' (of love) she has caused
    others to suffer
    simply absolutely
77 *friend* lover. See II.i.153n.
79 *breed teeth* cut his teeth, i.e. the Duke will soon show his teeth
81 *great one* the Duke; or perhaps the Devil   83 *course* pack (of dogs); flow

To their eternal kennels. I speak softly now –
'Tis manners in a noble woman's lodgings,   85
And I well know all my degrees of duty –
But come I to your everlasting parting once,
Thunder shall seem soft music to that tempest.
BIANCA
'Twas said last week there would be change of weather,
When the moon hung so, and belike you heard it.   90
LEANTIO
Why, here's sin made, and nev'r a conscience put to't;
A monster with all forehead and no eyes!
Why do I talk to thee of sense or virtue,
That art as dark as death? And as much madness
To set light before thee, as to lead blind folks   95
To see the monuments, which they may smell as soon
As they behold; marry, oft-times their heads
For want of light may feel the hardness of 'em.
So shall thy blind pride my revenge and anger,
That canst not see it now; and it may fall   100
At such an hour when thou least seest of all;
So to an ignorance darker than thy womb,
I leave thy perjured soul. A plague will come!   *Exit*
BIANCA
Get you gone first, and then I fear no greater,
Nor thee will I fear long; I'll have this sauciness   105
Soon banished from these lodgings and the rooms
Perfumed well after the corrupt air it leaves.
His breath has made me almost sick, in troth.
A poor base start-up! Life! Because h'as got
Fair clothes by foul means, comes to rail, and show
    'em.   110

                    Enter the DUKE
DUKE
Who's that?
BIANCA   Cry you mercy, sir.
DUKE   Prithee, who's that?
BIANCA
The former thing, my lord, to whom you gave
The captainship; he eats his meat with grudging still.

---

86 *know* ed. (knew O)
90 *moon hung* perhaps a reference to the crescent or horned (= cuckold) moon
91 *put to't* troubled
92 *forehead* front; impudence
96 *monuments* an unwitting allusion to the scene of Bianca's fall
101 *when . . . all* when she can least 'see' sin, i.e. in the 'dark' world of sexual betrayal

DUKE
  Still!
BIANCA   He comes vaunting here of his new love,
  And the new clothes she gave him: Lady Livia.   115
  Who but she now his mistress?
DUKE   Lady Livia?
  Be sure of what you say.
BIANCA   He showed me her name, sir,
  In perfumed paper, her vows, her letter,
  With an intent to spite me; so his heart said,
  And his threats made it good – they were as spiteful   120
  As ever malice uttered, and as dangerous,
  Should his hand follow the copy.
DUKE   But that must not.
  Do not you vex your mind; prithee to bed, go.
  All shall be well and quiet.
BIANCA   I love peace, sir.
DUKE
  And so do all that love; take you no care for't,   125
  It shall be still provided to your hand.
                                        Exit [BIANCA]
  Who's near us there?

                    Enter MESSENGER

MESSENGER   My lord?
DUKE   Seek out Hippolito,
  Brother to Lady Livia, with all speed.
MESSENGER
  He was the last man I saw, my lord.   *Exit*
DUKE   Make haste.
  He is a blood soon stirred, and as he's quick   130
  To apprehend a wrong, he's bold and sudden
  In bringing forth a ruin. I know likewise
  The reputation of his sister's honour's
  As dear to him as life-blood to his heart;
  Beside, I'll flatter him with a goodness to her   135
  Which I now thought on, but nev'r meant to practise –

114 *vaunting* boasting
122 *Should . . . copy* should he imitate the model in his copybook, i.e. should he follow
    his threats ('malice') with action
130 *blood soon stirred* a young man easily aroused
131 *sudden* impetuous
132 *ruin* disastrous result
133 *honour's* ed. (honor O)
135 *goodness* benefit

Because I know her base – and that wind drives him.
The ulcerous reputation feels the poise
Of lightest wrongs, as sores are vexed with flies.
He comes.

Enter HIPPOLITO

          Hippolito, welcome.
HIPPOLITO   My loved lord.   140
DUKE
How does that lusty widow, thy kind sister?
Is she not sped yet of a second husband?
A bed-fellow she has, I ask not that;
I know she's sped of him.
HIPPOLITO   Of him, my lord?
DUKE
Yes, of a bed-fellow. Is the news so strange to you?   145
HIPPOLITO
I hope 'tis so to all.
DUKE   I wish it were, sir;
But 'tis confessed too fast. Her ignorant pleasures,
Only by lust instructed, have received
Into their services an impudent boaster,
One that does raise his glory from her shame,   150
And tells the midday sun what's done in darkness;
Yet blinded with her appetite, wastes her wealth,
Buys her disgraces at a dearer rate
Than bounteous housekeepers purchase their honour.
Nothing sads me so much, as that in love   155
To thee and to thy blood, I had picked out
A worthy match for her, the great Vincentio,
High in our favour and in all men's thoughts.
HIPPOLITO
Oh thou destruction of all happy fortunes,
Unsated blood! Know you the name, my lord,   160
Of her abuser?
DUKE   One Leantio.

137 *that wind drives him* i.e. the thought of her benefit will urge him on (as wind fills
     the sails of a ship)
138 *poise* weight
142 *sped yet of* yet furnished with
     second husband Actually, it would be her third; cf. I.ii.50.
147 *confessed too fast* admitted too openly
152 *wastes* i.e. she wastes
153 *dearer* higher, greater
156 *blood* family
160 *blood* sexual appetite

HIPPOLITO
  He's a factor!
DUKE   He nev'r made so brave a voyage
  By his own talk.
HIPPOLITO   The poor old widow's son!
  I humbly take my leave.
DUKE [*Aside*]   I see 'tis done.
  [*To him*] Give her good counsel, make her see her error;   165
  I know she'll hearken to you.
HIPPOLITO   Yes, my lord,
  I make no doubt, as I shall take the course
  Which she shall never know till it be acted;
  And when she wakes to honour, then she'll thank me
      for't.
  I'll imitate the pities of old surgeons   170
  To this lost limb, who ere they show their art
  Cast one asleep, then cut the diseased part.
  So out of love to her I pity most,
  She shall not feel him going till he's lost;
  Then she'll commend the cure.   *Exit*
DUKE   The great cure's past.   175
  I count this done already; his wrath's sure,
  And speaks an injury deep. Farewell, Leantio;
  This place will never hear thee murmur more.

       Enter LORD CARDINAL *attended* [*by* SERVANTS]

  Our noble brother, welcome!
CARDINAL   Set those lights down.
  Depart till you be called.
                                   [*Exeunt* SERVANTS]
DUKE [*Aside*]   There's serious business   180
  Fixed in his look; nay, it inclines a little
  To the dark colour of a discontentment.
  [*To him*] Brother, what is't commands your eye so
      powerfully?
  Speak, you seem lost.
CARDINAL   The thing I look on seems so
  To my eyes, lost for ever.
DUKE   You look on me.   185
CARDINAL
  What a grief 'tis to a religious feeling
  To think a man should have a friend so goodly,

170 *old surgeons* reference to early uses of anaesthesia during surgery
184 *lost* i.e. lost in thought

So wise, so noble, nay, a duke, a brother,
And all this certainly damned?
DUKE   How!
CARDINAL   'Tis no wonder,
If your great sin can do't. Dare you look up   190
For thinking of a vengeance? Dare you sleep,
For fear of never waking, but to death?
And dedicate unto a strumpet's love
The strength of your affections, zeal and health?
Here you stand now; can you assure your pleasures   195
You shall once more enjoy her, but once more?
Alas, you cannot; what a misery 'tis, then,
To be more certain of eternal death
Than of a next embrace! Nay, shall I show you
How more unfortunate you stand in sin,   200
Than the low private man? All his offences,
Like enclosed grounds, keep but about himself,
And seldom stretch beyond his own soul's bounds;
And when a man grows miserable, 'tis some comfort
When he's no further charged than with himself;   205
'Tis a sweet ease to wretchedness. But, great man,
Ev'ry sin thou commit'st shows like a flame
Upon a mountain; 'tis seen far about,
And with a big wind made of popular breath
The sparkles fly through cities. Here one takes,   210
Another catches there, and in short time
Waste all to cinders. But remember still,
What burnt the valleys, first came from the hill.
Ev'ry offence draws his particular pain,
But 'tis example proves the great man's bane.   215
The sins of mean men lie like scattered parcels
Of an unperfect bill; but when such fall,
Then comes example, and that sums up all.
And this your reason grants: if men of good lives,
Who by their virtuous actions stir up others   220
To noble and religious imitation,
Receive the greater glory after death –

201 *low* ed. (love O)
202 *enclosed grounds* fenced-off land
205 *charged* burdened
209 *popular breath* the words or gossip of common people
214 *draws* brings with it, produces
215 *example* i.e. being an example
215–18 *great man ... all* i.e. the sins of common men are like isolated items of an
      incomplete bill, but when 'great' men fall (or die), their sins are gathered together
      under the heading of 'example', and all such are then so judged

As sin must needs confess – what may they feel
In height of torments and in weight of vengeance,
Not only they themselves not doing well,   225
But sets a light up to show men to Hell?
DUKE
If you have done, I have. No more, sweet brother.
CARDINAL
I know time spent in goodness is too tedious;
This had not been a moment's space in lust, now.
How dare you venture on eternal pain   230
That cannot bear a minute's reprehension?
Methinks you should endure to hear that talked of
Which you so strive to suffer. Oh my brother!
What were you, if you were taken now?
My heart weeps blood to think on't; 'tis a work 235
Of infinite mercy you can never merit
That yet you are not death-struck, no, not yet.
I dare not stay you long, for fear you should not
Have time enough allowed you to repent in.
There's but this wall betwixt you and destruction 240
When y'are at strongest, and but poor thin clay.
Think upon't, brother. Can you come so near it
For a fair strumpet's love, and fall into
A torment that knows neither end nor bottom
For beauty, but the deepness of a skin,   245
And that not of their own neither? Is she a thing
Whom sickness dare not visit, or age look on,
Or death resist? Does the worm shun her grave?
If not – as your soul knows it – why should lust
Bring man to lasting pain, for rotten dust?   250
DUKE
Brother of spotless honour, let me weep
The first of my repentance in thy bosom,
And show the blest fruits of a thankful spirit;
And if I e'er keep woman more unlawfully,
May I want penitence at my greatest need –   255
And wise men know there is no barren place
Threatens more famine, than a dearth in grace.

231 *reprehension* rebuke
234 *taken* i.e. taken by death
238 *stay* delay
240–1 *wall . . . clay* conventional metaphors for the frailty of the body
246 *not of their own* i.e. produced by cosmetics
255 *want* lack

CARDINAL
Why, here's a conversion is at this time, brother,
Sung for a hymn in Heaven; and at this instant
The powers of darkness groan, makes all Hell sorry.   260
First, I praise Heaven; then in my work I glory.
Who's there attends without?

Enter SERVANTS

SERVANT   My lord.
CARDINAL
Take up those lights; there was a thicker darkness
When they came first. The peace of a fair soul
Keep with my noble brother.
                    Exit [LORD] CARDINAL [*and* SERVANTS]
DUKE   Joys be with you, sir.   265
She lies alone tonight for't, and must still,
Though it be hard to conquer; but I have vowed
Never to know her as a strumpet more,
And I must save my oath. If fury fail not,
Her husband dies tonight, or at the most   270
Lives not to see the morning spent tomorrow;
Then will I make her lawfully mine own,
Without this sin and horror. Now I'm chidden
For what I shall enjoy then unforbidden,
And I'll not freeze in stoves; 'tis but a while   275
Live like a hopeful bridegroom, chaste from flesh;
And pleasure then will seem new, fair and fresh.   *Exit*

258–9 *conversion ... Heaven* Cf. Luke 15:10: 'There is joy in the presence of the
    angels of God over one sinner that repenteth'.
267 *it* his desire
269 *save my oath* keep my word
275 *freeze in stoves* freeze in rooms where there is heat ('stoves' = rooms heated by
    hot air)

Act IV, Scene ii

Enter HIPPOLITO

HIPPOLITO
The morning so far wasted, yet his baseness
So impudent? See if the very sun do not blush at him!
Dare he do thus much, and know me alive!
Put case one must be vicious, as I know myself
Monstrously guilty, there's a blind time made for't;   5
He might use only that, 'twere conscionable.
Art, silence, closeness, subtlety, and darkness
Are fit for such a business. But there's no pity
To be bestowed on an apparent sinner,
An impudent daylight lecher! The great zeal   10
I bear to her advancement in this match
With Lord Vincentio, as the Duke has wrought it,
To the perpetual honour of our house,
Puts fire into my blood, to purge the air
Of this corruption, fear it spread too far,   15
And poison the whole hopes of this fair fortune.
I love her good so dearly, that no brother
Shall venture farther for a sister's glory
Than I for her preferment.

Enter LEANTIO *and a* PAGE

LEANTIO   Once again
I'll see that glist'ring whore shines like a serpent,   20
Now the court sun's upon her. Page!
PAGE   Anon, sir!
LEANTIO
I'll go in state too; see the coach be ready.
                                        [*Exit* PAGE]
I'll hurry away presently.
HIPPOLITO   Yes, you shall hurry,

---

4 *Put case* assuming
  vicious i.e. full of vice
6 *conscionable* scrupulous
7 *Art* artifice, cunning
  closeness secrecy
9 *apparent* open, obvious
15 *fear* for fear
20 *glist'ring ... serpent* She is 'glist'ring' and linked with the serpent (= devil)
   because she is in the 'court sun's' glare, and her new status and rich clothing
   reflect its light as a serpent's skin the sun.
22 LEANTIO This speech ascription comes before l. 23 in O.

And the devil after you; take that at setting forth!

[*Strikes* LEANTIO]

Now, and you'll draw, we are upon equal terms, sir.   25
Thou took'st advantage of my name in honour
Upon my sister; I nev'r saw the stroke
Come, till I found my reputation bleeding;
And therefore count it I no sin to valour
To serve thy lust so. Now we are of even hand,   30
Take your best course against me. You must die.

LEANTIO
How close sticks envy to man's happiness!
When I was poor and little cared for life,
I had no such means offered me to die,
No man's wrath minded me. [*Draws his sword*] Slave,
    I turn this to thee,   35
To call thee to account for a wound lately
Of a base stamp upon me.

HIPPOLITO   'Twas most fit
For a base mettle. Come and fetch one now
More noble, then, for I will use thee fairer
Than thou hast done thine own soul or our honour;   40
And there I think 'tis for thee.

[*They fight and* LEANTIO *falls*]

[VOICES] WITHIN   Help, help, oh part 'em!
LEANTIO
False wife! I feel now th'hast prayed heartily for me.
Rise, strumpet, by my fall, thy lust may reign now;
My heart-string and the marriage-knot that tied thee
Breaks both together. [*Dies*]
HIPPOLITO   There I heard the sound on't,   45
And never liked string better.

Enter GUARDIANO, LIVIA, ISABELLA, WARD,
            and SORDIDO

LIVIA   'Tis my brother!

24 *at setting forth* to begin with
25 *and* if
30 *of even hand* in an equal position
37 *base stamp* base nature; false impression on face of a coin
38 *base mettle* base disposition; base metal (linked to coin metaphor in previous line)
40 *own* ed. (*not in* O)
44 *heart-string* nerve or tendon supposed to sustain heart
46 *string* i.e. string of musical instrument

Are you hurt, sir?
HIPPOLITO   Not anything.
LIVIA   Blessed fortune!
   Shift for thyself; what is he thou hast killed?
HIPPOLITO
   Our honour's enemy.
GUARDIANO   Know you this man, lady?
LIVIA
   Leantio? My love's joy? [*To* HIPPOLITO] Wounds stick
      upon thee   50
   As deadly as thy sins! Art thou not hurt?
   The devil take that fortune. And he dead!
   Drop plagues into thy bowels without voice,
   Secret and fearful. [*To others*] Run for officers!
   Let him be apprehended with all speed,   55
   For fear he scape away; lay hands on him!
   We cannot be too sure, 'tis wilful murder!
   You do Heaven's vengeance and the law just service;
   You know him not as I do: he's a villain,
   As monstrous as a prodigy, and as dreadful.   60
HIPPOLITO
   Will you but entertain a noble patience
   Till you but hear the reason, worthy sister!
LIVIA
   The reason! That's a jest Hell falls a-laughing at!
   Is there a reason found for the destruction
   Of our more lawful loves? And was there none   65
   To kill the black lust 'twixt thy niece and thee
   That has kept close so long?
GUARDIANO   How's that, good madam?
LIVIA
   Too true, sir, there she stands, let her deny't;
   The deed cries shortly in the midwife's arms,
   Unless the parents' sins strike it still-born.   70
   And if you be not deaf and ignorant,
   You'll hear strange notes ere long. [*To* ISABELLA] Look
      upon me, wench!
   'Twas I betrayed thy honour subtly to him

---

48 *Shift for thyself* i.e. make your own escape
53 *without voice* silently, without warning
60 *prodigy* unnatural marvel
67 *close* secret
71 *ignorant* wilfully disregarding
72 *strange* new, unfamiliar

Under a false tale; it lights upon me now.
His arm has paid me home upon thy breast,   75
My sweet, beloved Leantio!
GUARDIANO   Was my judgement
And care in choice so dev'lishly abused,
So beyond shamefully? All the world will grin at me!
WARD
Oh Sordido, Sordido, I'm damned, I'm damned!
SORDIDO
Damned! Why, sir?
WARD   One of the wicked; dost not see't?   80
A cuckold, a plain reprobate cuckold!
SORDIDO
Nay, and you be damned for that, be of good cheer, sir,
y'have gallant company of all professions; I'll have a wife
next Sunday too, because I'll along with you myself.
WARD
That will be some comfort yet.   85
LIVIA
[*To* GUARDIANO] You, sir, that bear your load of injuries
As I of sorrows, lend me your grieved strength
To this sad burthen who, in life, wore actions
Flames were not nimbler. We will talk of things
May have the luck to break our hearts together.   90
GUARDIANO
I'll list to nothing but revenge and anger,
Whose counsels I will follow.
                              Exeunt LIVIA *and* GUARDIANO
                              [*carrying* LEANTIO's *body*]
SORDIDO   A wife, quoth'a!
Here's a sweet plum-tree of your guardianer's grafting!

74–5 *it ... breast* i.e. my treachery has been returned upon me
80–1 *see't? / A* ed. (see't, a O)
82–4 arranged as verse in O
84 *Sunday* when wives will be well-dressed and apparently virtuous, yet actually
   flirtatious with others. Proverbial misogyny: 'Who will have a handsome wife let
   him choose her upon Saturday and not upon Sunday' (Tilley, W 378).
88–9 *wore ... nimbler* i.e. was characterized by actions more energetic ('nimbler')
   than fire
91 *list* listen
92 *quoth'a* said he
93 *plum-tree* i.e. female genitals
   guardianer's a gardener's grafting of two unlike plants together; the guardian's
   marrying of two unlike people
   grafting ed. (graffing O)

WARD

Nay, there's a worse name belongs to this fruit yet, and
you could hit on't, a more open one. For he that marries   95
a whore looks like a fellow bound all his lifetime to a
medlar-tree; and that's good stuff, 'tis no sooner ripe but
it looks rotten – and so do some queans at nineteen. A
pox on't, I thought there was some knavery abroach, for
something stirred in her belly the first night I lay with   100
her.

SORDIDO

What, what, sir!

WARD

This is she brought up so courtly! Can sing, and dance,
and tumble too, methinks. I'll never marry wife again
that has so many qualities.   105

SORDIDO

Indeed they are seldom good, master. For likely when
they are taught so many, they will have one trick more
of their own finding out. Well, give me a wench but with
one good quality, to lie with none but her husband, and
that's bringing-up enough for any woman breathing.   110

WARD

This was the fault when she was tendered to me; you
never looked to this.

SORDIDO

Alas, how would you have me see through a great farthingale, sir! I cannot peep through a millstone, or in the
going, to see what's done i'th'bottom.   115

WARD

Her father praised her breast, sh'ad the voice, forsooth;

94–8 *worse . . . queans* not a 'plum-tree' but another kind of 'fruit' (= female genitals).
The 'more open one' is the 'medlar', a small pulpy apple, nearly 'rotten' as soon
as it is 'ripe'; because of these characteristics, reminiscent of the symptoms of
venereal disease, the medlar was frequently associated with the degenerate sexuality of 'queans' (whores). The 'open one' also alludes to the dialect name for
the medlar, 'open-arse'; see *Romeo and Juliet* II.i.39.

104 *tumble* do acrobatics; have sexual intercourse

105 *qualities* skills, accomplishments. Some writers of the time argued that (over-)
educated women were untrustworthy.

113–14 *farthingale* a framework of hoops, worn about the waist, which extended a
woman's dress

114 *peep . . . millstone* i.e. see acutely, resolve difficulties; proverbial (Tilley, M 965)

115 *going* walking (i.e. while she's walking)
    i'th'bottom at the bottom; at her genitals

116–19 arranged as verse in O

I marvelled she sung so small indeed, being no maid.
Now I perceive there's a young chorister in her belly –
this breeds a singing in my head, I'm sure.

SORDIDO
'Tis but the tune of your wives' cinquepace, danced in a   120
featherbed. 'Faith, go lie down, master – but take heed
your horns do not make holes in the pillowberes. [*Aside*]
I would not batter brows with him for a hogshead of
angels; he would prick my skull as full of holes as a
scrivener's sand-box.   125

Exeunt WARD *and* SORDIDO

ISABELLA
[*Aside*] Was ever maid so cruelly beguiled
To the confusion of life, soul, and honour,
All of one woman's murdering! I'd fain bring
Her name no nearer to my blood than woman,
And 'tis too much of that. Oh shame and horror!   130
In that small distance from yon man to me
Lies sin enough to make a whole world perish.
[*To him*] 'Tis time we parted, sir, and left the sight
Of one another; nothing can be worse
To hurt repentance, for our very eyes   135
Are far more poisonous to religion
Than basilisks to them. If any goodness
Rest in you, hope of comforts, fear of judgements,
My request is, I nev'r may see you more;
And so I turn me from you everlastingly,   140
So is my hope to miss you. But for her,
That durst so dally with a sin so dangerous,
And lay a snare so spitefully for my youth,
If the least means but favour my revenge,
That I may practise the like cruel cunning   145

117–18 *small ... chorister* i.e. he was surprised she sang so softly (perhaps also at a
    treble pitch) because she was no young girl. He now claims it was the unborn
    baby's voice.
119 *singing in my head* alleged symptom of cuckoldry
120 *cinquepace* galliard (a lively French dance)
122 *horns* cuckold's horns
    pillowberes pillowcases
123–4 *hogshead of angels* barrel of gold coins (an 'angel' coin had a picture of St
    Michael on one side)
125 *scrivener's sand-box* perforated box filled with sand, used for blotting ink
127 *confusion* ruin
129 *blood* kinship
137 *basilisks* mythical reptiles (part cock, part serpent), able to kill by their glance
141 *miss you* i.e. to avoid meeting him 'everlastingly', in Hell

Upon her life, as she has on mine honour,
I'll act it without pity.
HIPPOLITO   Here's a care
Of reputation and a sister's fortune
Sweetly rewarded by her. Would a silence,
As great as that which keeps among the graves,   150
Had everlastingly chained up her tongue;
My love to her has made mine miserable.

Enter GUARDIANO *and* LIVIA [*who talk aside*]

GUARDIANO
If you can but dissemble your heart's griefs now,
Be but a woman so far.
LIVIA   Peace! I'll strive, sir.
GUARDIANO
As I can wear my injuries in a smile,   155
Here's an occasion offered, that gives anger
Both liberty and safety to perform
Things worth the fire it holds, without the fear
Of danger or of law; for mischiefs acted
Under the privilege of a marriage-triumph   160
At the Duke's hasty nuptials will be thought
Things merely accidental; all's by chance,
Not got of their own natures.
LIVIA   I conceive you, sir,
Even to a longing for performance on't;
And here behold some fruits.

[*Kneels before* HIPPOLITO *and* ISABELLA]

                            Forgive me both.   165
What I am now, returned to sense and judgement,
Is not the same rage and distraction
Presented lately to you; that rude form
Is gone for ever. I am now myself,
That speaks all peace and friendship; and these tears 170
Are the true springs of hearty, penitent sorrow
For those foul wrongs which my forgetful fury
Slandered your virtues with. This gentleman

158–60 *fear ... marriage-triumph* i.e. the law would be suspended ('privilege' =
    legal immunity) during the 'marriage-triumph', the masque performed for the
    marriage. As Middleton notes in *The Revenger's Tragedy*: 'A masque is treason's
    licence: that build upon – / 'Tis murder's best face, when a vizard's on!' (V.i.177–
    8).
162 *all's* all as if
163–5 *got ... conceive ... longing ... fruits* These words also refer to conception and
    pregnancy.

Is well resolved now.
GUARDIANO   I was never otherways.
I knew, alas, 'twas but your anger spake it,   175
And I nev'r thought on't more.
HIPPOLITO   Pray rise, good sister.
ISABELLA
[*Aside*] Here's ev'n as sweet amends made for a wrong
    now
As one that gives a wound, and pays the surgeon;
All the smart's nothing, the great loss of blood,
Or time of hindrance. Well, I had a mother,   180
I can dissemble too. [*To* LIVIA] What wrongs have
    slipped
Through anger's ignorance, aunt, my heart forgives.
GUARDIANO
Why thus tuneful now!
HIPPOLITO   And what I did, sister,
Was all for honour's cause, which time to come
Will approve to you.
LIVIA   Being awaked to goodness,   185
I understand so much, sir, and praise now
The fortune of your arm, and of your safety;
For by his death y'have rid me of a sin
As costly as ev'r woman doted on.
T'has pleased the Duke so well, too, that – behold, sir – 190
H'as sent you here your pardon,

                    [*Gives him a letter*]

                            which I kissed
With most affectionate comfort; when 'twas brought,
Then was my fit just past; it came so well, methought,
To glad my heart.
HIPPOLITO   I see his grace thinks on me.
LIVIA
There's no talk now but of the preparation   195
For the great marriage.
HIPPOLITO   Does he marry her, then?
LIVIA
With all speed, suddenly, as fast as cost
Can be laid on with many thousand hands.

174 *resolved* satisfied, informed
180 *hindrance* incapacity
183 *thus* Many editors emend to 'this is', supplying the supposedly missing verb; but
    Guardiano's line could be either an exclamation or a suspicious question, since
    O frequently uses question-marks and exclamation-marks interchangeably.
185 *approve* prove, demonstrate

This gentleman and I had once a purpose
To have honoured the first marriage of the Duke   200
With an invention of his own; 'twas ready,
The pains well past, most of the charge bestowed on't;
Then came the death of your good mother, niece,
And turned the glory of it all to black.
'Tis a device would fit these times so well, too,   205
Art's treasury not better. If you'll join,
It shall be done, the cost shall all be mine.

HIPPOLITO
Y'have my voice first, 'twill well approve my thankful-
ness
For the Duke's love and favour.

LIVIA   What say you, niece?

ISABELLA
I am content to make one.

GUARDIANO   The plot's full, then;   210
Your pages, madam, will make shift for cupids.

LIVIA
That will they, sir.

GUARDIANO   You'll play your old part still.

LIVIA
What, is't good? Troth, I have ev'n forgot it.

GUARDIANO
Why, Juno Pronuba, the marriage-goddess.

LIVIA
'Tis right, indeed.

GUARDIANO [To ISABELLA] And you shall play the nymph   215
That offers sacrifice to appease her wrath.

ISABELLA
Sacrifice, good sir?

LIVIA   Must I be appeased, then?

GUARDIANO
That's as you list yourself, as you see cause.

---

201 *invention* literary composition
     his own Guardiano's
202 *pains* effort
     charge bestowed cost paid out
208 *voice* support
210 *make one* play a part
     plot's full the cast is complete; the revenge plot is ready
211 *make shift for* improvise as
214 *Juno Pronuba* Juno watched over the arrangement of marriages – a highly ironic
     role for Livia to be playing.
218 *list* choose

LIVIA
  Methinks 'twould show the more state in her deity
  To be incensed.
ISABELLA   'Twould, but my sacrifice   220
  Shall take a course to appease you, or I'll fail in't,
  [*Aside*] And teach a sinful bawd to play a goddess.
GUARDIANO
  For our parts, we'll not be ambitious, sir;
  Please you walk in and see the project drawn,
  Then take your choice.
HIPPOLITO   I weigh not, so I have one. *Exit* 225
LIVIA
  [*Aside*] How much ado have I to restrain fury
  From breaking into curses! Oh how painful 'tis
  To keep great sorrow smothered! Sure I think
  'Tis harder to dissemble grief than love.
  Leantio, here the weight of thy loss lies,   230
  Which nothing but destruction can suffice.
                              Exeunt

Act IV, Scene iii

Hoboys

Enter in great state the DUKE *and* BIANCA, *richly attired, with*
LORDS, CARDINALS, LADIES, *and other* ATTENDANTS; *they*
pass solemnly over. Enter LORD CARDINAL *in a rage, seeming*
to break off the ceremony

CARDINAL
  Cease, cease! Religious honours done to sin
  Disparage virtue's reverence, and will pull

219–20 *more ... incensed* i.e. she would seem more stately if she were angry. Mulryne
    also suggests an unwitting pun on incense (part of the 'sacrifice', l. 216), since
    Livia will be killed by poisoned incense.
224 *project drawn* the plan of the masque written out
225 *weigh* care
225 s.d. Many editions send everyone except Livia off the stage at this point, but
    Holdsworth (p. 90) offers a convincing argument that Hippolito's solitary exit in
    O suggests his new isolation.
s.d. 1 *Hoboys* oboes
s.d. 4 *they pass ... over* They enter the playhouse yard, ascend and cross over the
    stage, and then return to the yard to exit (cf. the opening stage directions to *The*
    Revenger's Tragedy); the Cardinal apparently halts the procession while it is still
    on stage.

Heaven's thunder upon Florence; holy ceremonies
Were made for sacred uses, not for sinful.
Are these the fruits of your repentance, brother?   5
Better it had been you had never sorrowed
Than to abuse the benefit, and return
To worse than where sin left you.
Vowed you then never to keep strumpet more,
And are you now so swift in your desires   10
To knit your honours and your life fast to her?
Is not sin sure enough to wretched man
But he must bind himself in chains to't? Worse!
Must marriage, that immaculate robe of honour,
That renders virtue glorious, fair, and fruitful   15
To her great Master, be now made the garment
Of leprosy and foulness? Is this penitence,
To sanctify hot lust? What is it otherways
Than worship done to devils? Is this the best
Amends that sin can make after her riots?   20
As if a drunkard, to appease Heaven's wrath,
Should offer up his surfeit for a sacrifice!
If that be comely, then lust's offerings are
On wedlock's sacred altar.
DUKE   Here y'are bitter
Without cause, brother. What I vowed, I keep   25
As safe as you your conscience, and this needs not.
I taste more wrath in't than I do religion,
And envy more than goodness. The path now
I tread is honest, leads to lawful love,
Which virtue in her strictness would not check.   30
I vowed no more to keep a sensual woman:
'Tis done; I mean to make a lawful wife of her.
CARDINAL
He that taught you that craft,
Call him not master long, he will undo you.
Grow not too cunning for your soul, good brother.   35
Is it enough to use adulterous thefts,
And then take sanctuary in marriage?
I grant, so long as an offender keeps
Close in a privileged temple, his life's safe;

17 *leprosy* often associated with syphilis. Cf. II.ii.425.
22 *surfeit* over-indulgence; vomit
23 *comely* decent
26 *this needs not* this reproach is unnecessary
31 *keep a sensual woman* woman kept for sensual purposes
33 *He* i.e. the Devil

But if he ever venture to come out, 40
And so be taken, then he surely dies for't.
So now y'are safe; but when you leave this body,
Man's only privileged temple upon earth,
In which the guilty soul takes sanctuary,
Then you'll perceive what wrongs chaste vows endure, 45
When lust usurps the bed that should be pure.

BIANCA
Sir, I have read you over all this while
In silence, and I find great knowledge in you,
And severe learning; yet 'mongst all your virtues
I see not charity written, which some call 50
The first-born of religion, and I wonder
I cannot see't in yours. Believe it, sir,
There is no virtue can be sooner missed
Or later welcomed; it begins the rest,
And sets 'em all in order. Heaven and angels 55
Take great delight in a converted sinner;
Why should you, then, a servant and professor,
Differ so much from them? If ev'ry woman
That commits evil should be therefore kept
Back in desires of goodness, how should virtue 60
Be known and honoured? From a man that's blind
To take a burning taper, 'tis no wrong,
He never misses it; but to take light
From one that sees, that's injury and spite.
Pray, whether is religion better served, 65
When lives that are licentious are made honest,
Than when they still run through a sinful blood?
'Tis nothing virtue's temples to deface;
But build the ruins, there's a work of grace.

DUKE
I kiss thee for that spirit; thou hast praised thy wit 70

42–3 *body . . . temple* In the Bible (I Corinthians 3:16), the body is the temple of the
    Holy Spirit – but it is not there a place in which a 'guilty soul' could take
    'sanctuary' (l. 44).
47 *read you over* closely observed you
51–5 *first-born . . . begins . . . order* Cf. I Corinthians 13:13: 'And now abideth faith,
    hope, charity, these three; but the greatest of these is charity'.
57 *professor* one who professes knowledge (here, one who professes to be a Christian)
67 *Than* or
    blood desire
69 *build the ruins* i.e. restore Bianca's virtue by marrying her

A modest way. On, on there!

Hoboys

CARDINAL   Lust is bold,
And will have vengeance speak, ere't be controlled.

Exeunt

Act V, Scene i

Enter GUARDIANO *and* WARD

GUARDIANO
Speak, hast thou any sense of thy abuse?
Dost thou know what wrong's done thee?
WARD   I were an ass
else.
I cannot wash my face, but I am feeling on't.
GUARDIANO
Here, take this galtrop, then; convey it secretly
Into the place I showed you. Look you, sir,   5
This is the trap-door to't.
WARD
I know't of old, uncle, since the last triumph; here rose
up a devil with one eye, I remember, with a company of
fireworks at's tail.
GUARDIANO
Prithee leave squibbing now, mark me and fail not; but   10
when thou hear'st me give a stamp, down with't. The
villain's caught then.
WARD
If I miss you, hang me; I love to catch a villain, and your
stamp shall go current, I warrant you. But how shall I

---

72 *controlled* put down, checked
3 *feeling on't* i.e. feeling the cuckold's horns
4 *galtrop* The caltrop was a weapon made with four spikes, so that one always
  stands upright; used primarily against cavalry.
6 *trap-door* a standard feature of the Elizabethan/Jacobean stage
7 *triumph* pageant
8–9 *devil ... fireworks* The stage-devil, usually a comic figure, was often
  accompanied by fireworks.
10 *squibbing* foolish talk; also pun on 'squib' (= firecracker)
13 *miss you* miss your signal; but also ironic foreshadowing
14 *stamp ... current* The stamp of your foot will be understood as valid; also pun on
  'stamp' = design impressed on coin.

    rise up and let him down too, all at one hole? That will   15
    be a horrible puzzle. You know I have a part in't, I play
    Slander.
GUARDIANO
    True, but never make you ready for't.
WARD
    No? My clothes are bought and all, and a foul fiend's
    head with a long contumelious tongue i'th'chaps on't,   20
    a very fit shape for Slander i'th'out-parishes.
GUARDIANO
    It shall not come so far, thou understand'st it not.
WARD
    Oh, oh!
GUARDIANO
    He shall lie deep enough ere that time, and stick first
    upon those.   25
WARD
    Now I conceive you, guardianer.
GUARDIANO
    Away, list to the privy stamp, that's all thy part.
WARD
    Stamp my horns in a mortar if I miss you, and give the
    powder in white wine to sick cuckolds – a very present
    remedy for the headache.   *Exit*   30
GUARDIANO
    If this should any way miscarry now –
    As, if the fool be nimble enough, 'tis certain –
    The pages that present the swift-winged Cupids
    Are taught to hit him with their shafts of love,
    Fitting his part, which I have cunningly poisoned.   35
    He cannot 'scape my fury; and those ills
    Will be laid all on fortune, not our wills.
    That's all the sport on't! For who will imagine
    That at the celebration of this night
    Any mischance that haps can flow from spite?   *Exit*   40

15 *rise up . . . let him down . . . at one hole* all with sexual connotations
20 *contumelious* offensive   *chaps* jaws
21 *out-parishes* parishes outside the boundaries of the City of London, where popular
    dramatic performances were legally tolerated. Morality-characters such as
    Slander might appear in such older plays.
24 *time, and* ed. (time, / And O)
25 *those* referring to the sharp points of the caltrop   27 *privy* secret
28–30 *Stamp . . . headache* The Ward proposes a medical remedy for cuckoldom (the
    'headache' of the horns), by mixing powdered 'horns' with white wine (a common
    base for mixing medicines).
33 *present* act

Act V, Scene ii

Flourish. Enter above DUKE, BIANCA, LORD CARDINAL,
FABRITIO, *and other* CARDINALS, LORDS *and* LADIES *in state*

DUKE
Now our fair duchess, your delight shall witness
How y'are beloved and honoured: all the glories
Bestowed upon the gladness of this night
Are done for your bright sake.
BIANCA   I am the more
In debt, my lord, to loves and courtesies   5
That offer up themselves so bounteously
To do me honoured grace, without my merit.
DUKE
A goodness set in greatness! How it sparkles
Afar off like pure diamonds set in gold!
How perfect my desires were, might I witness   10
But a fair noble peace 'twixt your two spirits!
The reconcilement would be more sweet to me
Than longer life to him that fears to die.
[*To* LORD CARDINAL] Good Sir!
CARDINAL   I profess peace, and am
content.
DUKE
I'll see the seal upon't, and then 'tis firm.   15
CARDINAL
You shall have all you wish. [*Kisses* BIANCA]
DUKE   I have all indeed now.
BIANCA
[*Aside*] But I have made surer work; this shall not blind
     me.
He that begins so early to reprove,
Quickly rid him or look for little love.
Beware a brother's envy; he's next heir too.   20
Cardinal, you die this night, the plot's laid surely:
In time of sports death may steal in securely;

---

s.d. *Flourish* i.e. of trumpets
  7 *grace ... merit* A specifically Protestant theological point – quite ironic coming
     from Bianca at this point, but the rhetorics of courtesy and religion are cynically
     deployed throughout the play.
 10 *perfect* complete
 15 *seal* Documents were sealed with wax and impressed with a coat of arms or other
     insignia.
 19 *rid* get rid of
 22–3 *securely; / Then* ed. (securely; then O)

Then 'tis least thought on.
For he that's most religious, holy friend,
Does not at all hours think upon his end;   25
He has his times of frailty, and his thoughts
Their transportations too, through flesh and blood,
For all his zeal, his learning, and his light,
As well as we poor souls that sin by night.

[FABRITIO *gives the* DUKE *a paper*]

DUKE
What's this, Fabritio?
FABRITIO   Marry, my lord, the model   30
Of what's presented.
DUKE   Oh we thank their loves;
Sweet duchess, take your seat, list to the argument.
Reads
There is a nymph that haunts the woods and springs,
In love with two at once, and they with her.
Equal it runs; but to decide these things,   35
The cause to mighty Juno they refer,
She being the marriage-goddess. The two lovers,
They offer sighs; the nymph a sacrifice;
All to please Juno, who by signs discovers
How the event shall be; so that strife dies.   40
Then springs a second; for the man refused
Grows discontent, and out of love abused
He raises Slander up, like a black fiend,
To disgrace th'other, which pays him i'th'end.
BIANCA
In troth, my lord, a pretty, pleasing argument,   45
And fits th'occasion well: Envy and Slander
Are things soon raised against two faithful lovers;
But comfort is, they are not long unrewarded.

Music

DUKE
This music shows they're upon entrance now.

27 *transportations* transports, raptures
29 *we poor souls* ed. (we, poor soul, O)
30 *model* outline, plan
32 *argument* plot summary
39 *discovers* reveals
40 *event* outcome
44 *pays him* brings an appropriate revenge on him

BIANCA
  [*Aside*] Then enter all my wishes!   50

Enter HYMEN *in yellow,* GANYMEDE *in a blue robe powdered
with stars, and* HEBE *in a white robe with golden stars, with
covered cups in their hands. They dance a short dance, then
bowing to the* DUKE, *&c.* HYMEN *speaks*

HYMEN
  [*Giving* BIANCA *a cup*] « To thee, fair bride, Hymen
    offers up
  Of nuptial joys this the celestial cup.
  Taste it, and thou shalt ever find
  Love in thy bed, peace in thy mind. »
BIANCA
  We'll taste you, sure, 'twere pity to disgrace   55
  So pretty a beginning.
DUKE   'Twas spoke nobly.
GANYMEDE
  « Two cups of nectar have we begged from Jove;
  Hebe give that to innocence, I this to love.

          [HEBE *gives a cup to the* LORD CARDINAL,
            GANYMEDE *one to the* DUKE; *both drink*]

  Take heed of stumbling more, look to your way;
  Remember still the Via Lactea. »   60
HEBE
  « Well, Ganymede, you have more faults, though not
    so known;
  I spilled one cup, but you have filched many a one. »
HYMEN
  « No more, forbear for Hymen's sake;
  In love we met, and so let's parting take. »

50 s.d. 1 *HYMEN* the god of marriage, traditionally represented in yellow robes
     s.d. 1–2 *GANYMEDE* cupbearer to Zeus (Jove). The 'stars' indicate that Zeus
     stellified him.
     s.d. 2–3 *HEBE* daughter of Zeus, once cupbearer to Zeus
58 s.d. The Yale copy of O has this manuscript annotation here: 'To the Duke the
     wrong cup by mistake'.
59 *stumbling more* Mulryne identifies the source as William Fulke, *A goodly gallerye*
     ... (1563): '*Hebe*, one which was *Iupiter's* Cupbearer, on a tyme stombled at a
     starre, and shedde the wyne or mylke, that was in the cuppe, which colloured
     that part of heaven to this daye, wherfore she was pout out of her office' (E6v);
     he has also found this myth in E.K.'s gloss on l. 195 of the November Eclogue in
     Spenser's *Shepherd's Calendar*.
60 *Via Lactea* the Milky Way
64 *parting take* ed. (part O). A rhyme with 'sake' seems called for here.

Exeunt [HYMEN, GANYMEDE, *and* HEBE]

DUKE

But soft! Here's no such persons in the argument   65
As these three, Hymen, Hebe, Ganymede.
The actors that this model here discovers
Are only four, Juno, a nymph, two lovers.

BIANCA

This is some antemasque belike, my lord,
To entertain time. [*Aside*] Now my peace is perfect.   70
[*To* DUKE] Let sports come on apace; now is their
    time, my lord.

Music

Hark you, you hear from 'em!

DUKE   The nymph indeed!

Enter two dressed like nymphs, bearing two tapers lighted; then
ISABELLA *dressed with flowers and garlands, bearing a censer*
with fire in it; they set the censer and tapers on JUNO's *altar*
with much reverence; this ditty being sung in parts

Ditty

Juno, nuptial-goddess,
Thou that rul'st o'er coupled bodies,
Tiest man to woman, never to forsake her,   75
Thou only powerful marriage-maker,
Pity this amazed affection;
I love both, and both love me;
Nor know I where to give rejection,
My heart likes so equally,   80
Till thou set'st right my peace of life,
And with thy power conclude this strife.

65 *argument* The Duke comments throughout the scene on the discrepancies
    between the 'argument' (ll. 32, 65) or 'plot' (l. 129) of the masque which he is
    reading and the action before him.
69 *antemasque* a brief, often comic, interlude before the masque proper; here, just
    Bianca's cover story
70 *perfect* complete
72 s.d. 5 *in parts* sung separately, not in unison
73–4 *goddess, / Thou* ed. (Goddess, thou O)
75 *Tiest* ed. (Ty'st O)
75–6 *her, / Thou* ed. (her, thou O)
77 *amazed* perplexed, bewildered
77–8 *affection; / I* ed. (affection; I O)
79–80 *rejection, / My* ed. (rejection, my O)

ISABELLA
  [*To* NYMPHS] « Now with my thanks depart you to the
      springs,
  I to these wells of love.
                              [*Exeunt the two* NYMPHS]
                        Thou sacred goddess,
  And queen of nuptials, daughter to great Saturn,   85
  Sister and wife to Jove, imperial Juno,
  Pity this passionate conflict in my breast,
  This tedious war 'twixt two affections;
  Crown one with victory, and my heart's at peace. »

                Enter HIPPOLITO *and* GUARDIANO,
                          like shepherds

HIPPOLITO
  « Make me that happy man, thou mighty goddess. »   90
GUARDIANO
  « But I live most in hope, if truest love
      Merit the greatest comfort. »
ISABELLA   « I love both
      With such an even and fair affection,
  I know not which to speak for, which to wish for,
  Till thou, great arbitress 'twixt lover's hearts,   95
  By thy auspicious grace, design the man;
  Which pity I implore. »
BOTH [HIPPOLITO *and* GUARDIANO]
                              « We all implore it. »
ISABELLA
  « And after sighs, contrition's truest odours,

                LIVIA *descends like* JUNO
              [*attended by* CUPIDS *with bows*]

  I offer to thy powerful deity,
  This precious incense, may it ascend peacefully. »   100

                [*Poisoned smoke rises*]

  [*Aside*] And if it keep true touch, my good aunt Juno,

---

83 *springs* where the nymphs live (cf. l. 33)
89 *one* ed. (me O)   96 *design* designate, point out
98 s.d. *Livia descends* Livia is lowered from the canopy overhead (the 'heavens'), a
    spectacular and highly popular stage effect utilized in many plays, including
    Jonson's *Masque of Hymenaei*, where Juno is lowered, and in Shakespeare's
    Cymbeline, where 'Jupiter descends in thunder and lightning, sitting upon an
    eagle' (V.iv.92 s.d.).
101 *keep true touch* prove trustworthy (from the testing of gold or silver with a
    'touchstone')

'Twill try your immortality ere't be long;
I fear you'll never get so nigh Heaven again,
When you're once down.

LIVIA   « Though you and your
    affections
Seem all as dark to our illustrious brightness   105
As night's inheritance, Hell, we pity you,
And your requests are granted. You ask signs;
They shall be given you, we'll be gracious to you.
He of those twain which we determine for you,
Love's arrows shall wound twice; the later wound   110
Betokens love in age: for so are all
Whose love continues firmly all their lifetime
Twice wounded at their marriage, else affection
Dies when youth ends. » [Aside] This savour overcomes
    me.
[As JUNO] « Now for a sign of wealth and golden days,   115
Bright-eyed prosperity which all couples love,
Ay, and makes love, take that!

            [Throws flaming gold upon ISABELLA,
                who falls dead]

                              Our brother Jove
Never denies us of his burning treasure,
T'express bounty. »

DUKE   She falls down upon't;
What's the conceit of that?

FABRITIO   As over-joyed, belike.   120
Too much prosperity overjoys us all,
And she has her lapful, it seems, my lord.

DUKE
This swerves a little from the argument, though.
Look you, my lords!

GUARDIANO
[Aside] All's fast; now comes my part to toll him hither;   125

105 *to* compared to
114 *savour* ed. (favor O); the odour of the poisoned incense
117 s.d. This stage direction derives from a manuscript annotation in the Yale copy
    of O. The allusion is to Jove's violation ('his burning treasure', l. 118) of Danae
    as a shower of gold; Isabella, like Danae, is overcome by a 'lapful' (l. 122) of 'too
    much prosperity' (l. 121). Juno's description in Jonson's *Masque of Hymenaei* is
    similar: 'Above her the *region of fire*, with a continual motion, was seen to whirl
    circularly'.
123 *argument* plot summary
125 *fast* i.e. secure, as planned
    toll him hither entice him to the trap-door; ring his death-knell

Then, with a stamp given, he's dispatched as cunningly.
HIPPOLITO
Stark dead! Oh treachery! Cruelly made away! How's
that?

[HIPPOLITO *angrily stamps on the floor upon discovering*
ISABELLA*'s body;* GUARDIANO *falls through the trap-door*]

FABRITIO
Look, there's one of the lovers dropped away too.
DUKE
Why sure, this plot's drawn false, here's no such thing.
LIVIA
Oh I am sick to th'death, let me down quickly;   130

[*She is lowered to the ground*]

This fume is deadly. Oh 't has poisoned me!
My subtlety is sped, her art has quitted me;
My own ambition pulls me down to ruin. [*Dies*]
HIPPOLITO
Nay, then I kiss thy cold lips, and applaud
This thy revenge in death.
FABRITIO   Look, Juno's down too.   135

CUPIDS *shoot* [*at* HIPPOLITO]

What makes she there? Her pride should keep aloft.
She was wont to scorn the earth in other shows.
Methinks her peacocks' feathers are much pulled.
HIPPOLITO
Oh death runs through my blood in a wild flame too!
Plague of those Cupids! Some lay hold on 'em.   140
Let 'em not 'scape, they have spoiled me; the shaft's
deadly.
DUKE
I have lost myself in this quite.
HIPPOLITO
My great lords, we are all confounded.
DUKE   How?

127 s.d. This stage direction is speculative; clearly, something goes wrong with
     Guardiano's plan, and he falls through his own trap. It may be that he himself
     stamps on the floor unwittingly, as most editions of the play suggest; or that he
     stamps on the floor when Hippolito is above the trap, nothing happens, and he
     goes to test the trap himself, with fatal consequences. I am following here G. B.
     Shand's useful suggestion, also adopted by Loughrey and Taylor.
132 *quitted me* requited me, paid me back
138 *peacock's feathers* Peacocks were sacred to Juno, according to Ovid.
141 *spoiled* destroyed

HIPPOLITO
  [*Points to* ISABELLA] Dead; and I worse.
FABRITIO   Dead? My girl
    dead? I hope
  My sister Juno has not served me so.   145
HIPPOLITO
  Lust and forgetfulness has been amongst us,
  And we are brought to nothing. Some blest charity
  Lend me the speeding pity of his sword
  To quench this fire in blood. Leantio's death
  Has brought all this upon us – now I taste it –   150
  And made us lay plots to confound each other.
  The event so proves it, and man's understanding
  Is riper at his fall than all his lifetime.
  She, in a madness for her lover's death,
  Revealed a fearful lust in our near bloods,   155
  For which I am punished dreadfully and unlooked for;
  Proved her own ruin too: vengeance met vengeance,
  Like a set match, as if the plagues of sin
  Had been agreed to meet here all together.
  But how her fawning partner fell, I reach not,   160
  Unless caught by some springe of his own setting –
  For on my pain, he never dreamed of dying;
  The plot was all his own, and he had cunning
  Enough to save himself. But 'tis the property
  Of guilty deeds to draw your wise men downward.   165
  Therefore the wonder ceases. Oh this torment!
DUKE
  Our guard below there!

                Enter a LORD *with a* GUARD

LORD   My lord.
HIPPOLITO   Run and meet death
    then,

---

144 *I worse* because the poison's pain is agonizing; because he also committed incest
152 *event* outcome
158 *Like a set match* as if by agreement
    plagues ed. (plague O)
159 *all together* ed. (altogether O)
160 *reach* understand
161 *springe* trap, snare
164 *property* quality, tendency

And cut off time and pain.

[Runs on a GUARD*'s halbert; dies]*

LORD   Behold my lord,
H'as run his breast upon a weapon's point.

DUKE
Upon the first night of our nuptial honours   170
Destruction play her triumph, and great mischiefs
Mask in expected pleasures! 'Tis prodigious!
They're things most fearfully ominous: I like 'em not.
Remove these ruined bodies from our eyes.

[The bodies are taken away]

BIANCA
[Aside] Not yet, no change? When falls he to the earth?   175

LORD
Please but your excellence to peruse that paper,
Which is a brief confession from the heart
Of him that fell first, ere his soul departed;
And there the darkness of these deeds speaks plainly.
'Tis the full scope, the manner, and intent;   180
His ward, that ignorantly let him down,
Fear put to present flight at the voice of him.

BIANCA
[Aside] Nor yet?

DUKE
[To LORD CARDINAL*]* Read, read; for I am lost in sight
    and strength.

CARDINAL
My noble brother!

BIANCA   Oh the curse of wretchedness!
My deadly hand is fall'n upon my lord.   185
Destruction take me to thee, give me way;
The pains and plagues of a lost soul upon him
That hinders me a moment!

168 s.d. *Runs ... dies* This stage direction derives from a manuscript annotation in
        the Yale copy of O.
        halbert not a sword, but a weapon with an axelike blade and a steel spike mounted
        on the end of a long shaft
168–9 *lord,* / *H'as* ed. (Lord, h'as O)
171 *triumph* pageant
172 *Mask in* wear a mask as
        prodigious ill-omened
178 *him* refers to Guardiano
181 *ignorantly* unintentionally, unwittingly
182 *present* immediate

DUKE
My heart swells bigger yet; help here, break't ope,
My breast flies open next. [*Dies*]
BIANCA   Oh with the poison   190
That was prepared for thee, thee, Cardinal!
'Twas meant for thee.
CARDINAL   .   Poor prince!
BIANCA   Accursed error!
Give me thy last breath, thou infected bosom,
And wrap two spirits in one poisoned vapour.

[*Kisses the* DUKE's *lips*]

Thus, thus, reward thy murderer, and turn death   195
Into a parting kiss. My soul stands ready at my lips,
Ev'n vexed to stay one minute after thee.
CARDINAL
The greatest sorrow and astonishment
That ever struck the general peace of Florence
Dwells in this hour.
BIANCA   So my desires are satisfied,   200
I feel death's power within me!
Thou hast prevailed in something, cursed poison,
Though thy chief force was spent in my lord's bosom.
But my deformity in spirit's more foul;
A blemished face best fits a leprous soul.   205
What make I here? These are all strangers to me,
Not known but by their malice, now th'art gone,
Nor do I seek their pities.

[*She seizes the poisoned cup and drinks from it*]

CARDINAL   Oh restrain
Her ignorant wilful hand!
BIANCA   Now do; 'tis done.
Leantio, now I feel the breach of marriage   210
At my heart-breaking! Oh the deadly snares
That women set for women, without pity
Either to soul or honour! Learn by me
To know your foes. In this belief I die:
Like our own sex, we have no enemy, no enemy!   215

189–90 It was widely believed that as the moment of death approached, the body's
blood supply rushed to the heart, making it swell and seem (to the victim) about
to burst.
205 *blemished . . . soul* Even the small amount of poison she has taken from the Duke's
lips (ll. 195–6) has begun to eat into and deform her face, a suitable outward
sign of the inner 'leprous soul'.
209 *ignorant* deliberately unknowing

LORD
  See, my lord,
  What shift sh'as made to be her own destruction.
BIANCA
  Pride, greatness, honours, beauty, youth, ambition,
  You must all down together, there's no help for't.
  Yet this gladness is, that I remove,   220
  Tasting the same death in a cup of love. [*Dies*]
CARDINAL
  Sin, what thou art, these ruins show too piteously.
  Two kings on one throne cannot sit together,
  But one must needs down, for his title's wrong;
  So where lust reigns, that prince cannot reign long.   225
                             Exeunt

FINIS

220 *remove* i.e. die

Made in United States
North Haven, CT
23 November 2024

60840763R00088